A Way of ESCAPE

Neil T. Anderson

WITH RUSS RUMMER

HARVEST HOUSE PUBLISHERS
Eugene, Oregon 97402

A WAY OF ESCAPE

Copyright © 1994 by Harvest House Publishers
Eugene, Oregon 97402

Library of Congress Cataloging-in-Publication Data

Anderson, Neil T., 1942–
    A way of escape / Neil T. Anderson.
      p.   cm.
    ISBN 1-56507-170-0
      1. Lust—Religious aspects—Christianity. 2. Sex—Religious aspects—Christianity. 3. Sex addiction—Religious aspects—Christianity. 4. Pastoral counseling.
5. Christian life. I. Title
BV4627.L8A53   1994   94-11042
241'.66—dc20   CIP

Printed in the United States of America.

94 95 96 97 98 99 00 01 — 10 9 8 7 6 5 4 3 2 1

Foreword

I wish that this powerful book were mine when I was going through my own savage struggle with lustful thoughts. For years they plagued my mind and irritated my soul. I tried everything I thought a Christian should try—Bible study and memorization, new experiences with God, and efforts at self-discipline, but nothing seemed to work for long.

I prayed during those times of struggle, too—God knows I prayed. I repented and turned away from my sins more often than I can remember. God answered my prayer at the moment. But the lustful thoughts always came back. Although I did not fall into an adulterous affair and avoided pornography like the plague, lust was the battleground of my Christian experience. I took three steps forward and two steps back, then two steps forward and three steps back, and then one step forward and four steps back.

Yes, there were holy-ground moments of fresh victory before God. I loved them. But then came the agonizing weeks and months of defeat. I hated them and hated my sin, yet could not escape it. Romans 7 describes my experience perfectly. I studied Romans 6 and 8 and tried to apply it. Somehow it worked in every area of my life except one. I could not seem to live constantly in the Spirit when it came to lust. There was something compulsive about my thought life that felt abnormal to me. Little did I know how real the spiritual problem really was.

During these years of silent, hidden struggle I felt I had no one to talk to. Later I figured out that there was no one I *wanted* to talk to. My pride and my shame almost did me in. I have already described my turning point in my book, *Running the Red Lights*. It was effective in setting me free in Christ, but now I know that it was unnecessary for me to have waited so long. If I had had this book back then, Christ would have set me free years sooner.

The simple insight of renouncing every sexual use of my body and mind outside of marriage proved so helpful when I first heard it. My temptations were much more normal by this time, and the compulsiveness was already broken. Nevertheless, as I asked Christ to bring to my mind each instance of sexual sin, three vivid memories popped into my thoughts. Each one was, I now believe, a foothold Satan and his demons used to form a stronghold in my mind. Renouncing each one led to greater freedom and joy than ever before.

In the days of my greatest struggle I did not know about the activity of Satan in putting his evil thoughts in my mind. I did not know my true identity as a man who was crucified, buried, made alive, raised up, and seated with Christ (Galatians 2:20; Romans 6:4; Ephesians 2:4-6). I did not know how to apply God's grace and truth to take every thought captive in obedience to Christ. I did not understand the authority and influence over the evil one that is mine in Christ. The Lord did teach me many lessons about becoming a winner and overcoming lust, but it would have been easier to become free if this book were in my hand years ago.

Most Christians desperately need the message of this book, either for their present struggle or for something in their past that has not been resolved. Any good book is like a cherry pie. Some readers will always find a theological pit and then be tempted to throw away the whole pie. Please don't do that. The message of this book has the potential to show how Christ can set millions of people free from sexual bondage. Read it, pass it on, and spread the word.

—Dr. Charles Mylander
Superintendent of the
Friends Church Southwest

Acknowledgments

The time it took to write this book was but a fraction of time I have spent with hurting people. Most have been victims of sexual abuse, and many have been carried away by their own lusts, enticed by a world spiraling out of control into a cesspool of sexual madness. Some had become abusers, while others degenerated into deviant sexual behaviors. They all bore the shame of a defiled temple and cowered under the accusation of the evil one.

If you saw only their behavior, you would never let your son or daughter marry one of them or let your children be around them. Ironically, they *are* your sons and daughters, other family members, friends, and coworkers. If you heard their story you would weep with them. Perhaps you are weeping now, because you know this book is for you. I want to acknowledge all of you who had the courage to face the truth and find the way of escape. Your willingness to share with me may have been motivated by desperation, but your story has helped shape my life and has driven me to search the Scriptures for the only hope for sexual freedom.

I also want to thank Dr. Robert Saucy for his wonderfully guided theological mind and helpful suggestions. I thank Dr. Charles Mylander for his feedback and his thoughtful comments in the Foreword. I appreciate your friendship and support of our ministry more than words can express.

I am especially grateful to Russ Rummer, a dear colleague in ministry, for his extensive contributions to this book. Some of the illustrations and insights have come from his many hours of counseling people who struggle in sexual bondage. Russ, you are a highly valued and much appreciated member of the Freedom In Christ staff.

Again I am indebted to the editorial contribution of Ed Stewart. Ed, your gift of writing is a gift to the Church. Special thanks to Barb Sherrill and Eileen Mason, who were a delight to work with, as was the entire crew at Harvest House. I am also grateful for my faithful staff at Freedom In Christ Ministries, who filled in for me during my absence and stood behind this project in prayer.

The actual credit goes to the Lord, who is the way of escape. He first delivered me from my own struggles and enabled me to stand.

Finally, I want to thank my wife, Joanne Anderson. You prayed for me, read my unedited first attempts, and generally put up with me. You are my helpmate, best friend, and confidante. I love you and dedicate this book to you, and I commit myself to be faithful to you until Christ calls me home.

—Neil

Contents

PART ONE

Detours into the Darkness

ONE

There Is a Way Out

Jon's problems with lust and sexual bondage literally began in a dumpster. That's where he came into contact with pornography for the first time as a boy. Curiously pawing through a trash bin on the military base where his father was stationed, Jon discovered more garbage than he had bargained for. Somehow he knew he should bury the dirty magazines and leave them there. But the lewd, tantalizing pictures captivated him. As Jon poured over the pages in secret wonder, the images burned into his mind. The hook was set.

Abruptly awakened to a sinister but exciting new world, young Jon began looking for other sources of stimulation. He soon discovered his father's stash of *Playboy* magazines and secretly returned to that hiding place often to fuel his unhealthy desires.

As he entered puberty, Jon became more adept at finding illicit material. He became entranced with sexual fantasy and frequent masturbation. With every experience, the grip of pornography on his mind strengthened. Jon's covert forays into the darker side of life also led him into experiments with alcohol, drugs, and sexual activity. Ironically, he retained the external image of a nice Christian boy. During high school he was active in Youth for Christ and involved in church, even though his parents did not attend.

When Jon turned 18, he enrolled in a Christian college. But his secret vices accelerated rapidly. His use of alcohol and drugs turned frightfully self-abusive. His uncontrolled desire to satisfy his sexual cravings escalated into the hard-core realm of pornographic movies. His focus in college turned from his studies to wild parties and sexual escapades. To his embarrassment, Jon ended up flunking out of school.

Hoping to find direction for his life by following his father into a military career, Jon joined the Navy. But things only got worse. Temptations to substance abuse and pornography seemed even more abundant. A random testing program uncovered Jon's drug problem, and he was repeatedly passed over for promotions.

Lying in the base hospital after a job-related injury, Jon came to the end of himself. He cried out to the Savior he had only pretended to serve during his youth and turned his miserable life over to Christ. The change was miraculous and instantaneous. His dependence on alcohol, drugs, and tobacco seemed to vanish. His desire for pornography and illicit sexual encounters was suddenly gone. Such peace at last!

But Jon's relief was short-lived. Three weeks later he chanced to find an enticing magazine in a rest room on the base. Yielding to the temptation, he began a new cycle of sin, guilt, and frustration. He was overwhelmed by shame at letting God down and plunging himself back into the mire of immorality. He knew of no one he could talk to who would understand his plight. He felt terribly alone.

After an honorable discharge from the Navy, Jon met and married Angela, a beautiful Christian woman who knew nothing of his sexual addiction. Hoping to appease the God he had disappointed, Jon returned to college, prepared for the ministry, and entered Christian service. Yet he remained in secret slavery to pornography and substance abuse. The inner conflict tortured him and his relationship with Angela with severe stress. He desperately yearned for something to break the destructive stranglehold he seemed powerless to escape.

Jon hoped the birth of their first child and a lucrative new job in sales was the answer. But business trips far from home only opened a new chapter for his sexual addiction. Pornographic movies were plentiful on the hotel cable channels, and printed material, cleverly hidden by previous guests, could be found in dozens of places in each room. Instead of finding release in his new position, Jon was further encouraged in the downward spiral of his bondage.

When Angela discovered the depth of Jon's problem and confronted him with it, he broke down and confessed everything. Angela forgave him and promised to stand with him through his recovery. Jon felt relieved at last to be free of the secrecy and to walk in the light of the truth.

But sadly, Jon didn't remain in the light for long. Soon he was back to his old destructive habits. Only this time Angela dropped a bomb. She would no longer tolerate the lies and selfish behavior that were ruining their family. After six years of marriage, she wanted a divorce—and she was determined to get it.

Jon suddenly realized that his dreams for a family and a lifetime of happiness were gone. His success in marriage, business, and Christian ministry had been torpedoed by a dark appetite he felt helpless to control. In despair, he flogged himself repeatedly with the thought, *If I had only left that garbage in the dumpster...*

An All-too-common Trap

Jon's sad experience as a Christian enslaved to lust and sinful habits is, unfortunately, neither an anomaly nor an isolated incident in our culture. I have talked to literally hundreds of individuals like Jon. Some of them come to me perplexed that their minds are constantly peppered by unholy thoughts related to sex. Others confess their failure to completely overcome sinful habits in this area which have stunted their daily victory and spiritual growth. Still others vent their secret agony at being slaves to uncontrollable lust and sexual immorality.

You may say, "You must be talking about unbelievers, especially when you mention people being slaves to sexual sin."

No, I'm not talking about unbelievers. The vast majority of the people I counsel are evangelical Christians attending churches like yours and mine. Many of them are in positions of service: teachers, choir members, committee members. Some are in positions of lay leadership: deacons, elders, board members. A surprising number of the people I deal with are even in full-time Christian ministry or in preparation for it: pastors, missionaries, officers in parachurch organizations, students at Bible college and seminary. It's very obvious to us that Christians at every level of growth and influence are vulnerable to temptation, bad habits, and bondage related to sex.

Sexual bondages are nearly as prevalent inside the church as they are outside. I surveyed the graduates of one of our country's better theological seminaries on the topic of sexual temptation. Sixty percent said they were feeling guilty about their sexual life. Nearly half of that 60 percent stated that they would sign up for an elective class for credit—if confidentiality could be ensured—which promised to help them find sexual freedom.

Several years ago a well-known Bible teacher presented a series of messages on sex in our seminary chapel. He urged students to get their sexual act together before they began their ministries. "We don't need another pastor falling into sexual immorality and bringing more embarrassment to the name of our Lord Jesus Christ," he exhorted. Recently this man lost his ministry due to sexual immorality.

Two Christian leaders who taught in our Doctor of Ministry program lost their ministries for the same reason. Many other Christian leaders have fallen. Some of them are friends of mine for whom I care deeply. And I am keenly aware that, apart from the grace of God, I also could end up like them. Don't be fooled: Christian people are not impervious to stumbling into sexual sin. And those who think they are beyond the range of the fiery dart of sexual immorality tend to be the ones most vulnerable to be pierced by it.

You may also be thinking, "You're surely talking about men here, not women. Unhealthy preoccupation and involvement with sex is a man thing."

No, I'm not only talking about men. Clearly, the masculine gender seems to be the primary target of Satan's assault on biblical morality, as evidenced by the tidal wave of pornography catering to men which floods the print and electronic media. But my experience has revealed that many women are also captivated by the lure of lustful fantasies and carnal activities.

Count the number of television soap operas in syndication—daytime dramas that cater to the fantasies of women. Consider some of the sleazy topics being discussed on the daytime talk shows. Notice the amount of shelf space in secular bookstores given to romance novels—those books with a bare-chested hunk and a swooning heroine entwined on the cover. Think about the increasing number of tabloids crowding the supermarket checkstands offering to tell all the juicy details about the immoral liaisons of Hollywood's hot stars.

Judging by the billions of dollars invested, there is clearly a huge market niche of women devouring this material. At every turn the biblical values of virginity, marital faithfulness, and even heterosexuality are being subtly or blatantly mocked. And sadly, many Christian women have been unwittingly sucked into this dark whirlpool of temptation to immorality—if only in their thoughts.

Like the Frog in the Kettle

When Jon first became involved with pornography, you could have asked him, "Do you intend to come under the control of this stuff?" He probably would have answered, "Of course not. I just want to look at it and think about it and enjoy it for a while. I won't let it control me." But when his life hit bottom many years later, he was forced to admit that what began as a titillating fascination had subtly enveloped him in its paralyzing tentacles. Jon had lost control and come into bondage to sex.

That's the ultimate destination of even the most "innocent" or insignificant sexual temptation which remains unchecked: loss of control, leading to sexual bondage. None of the men and women I have counseled ever intended their sexual fantasies to control them. But, like the proverbial frog in the kettle of water, they were unaware that their secret fascination with pornography or sexual fantasy was slowly cooking them into submission. Early in the process both the frog and the sexually tempted Christian are able to jump out of the hot water. But after continually compromising with and acclimating to their potentially deadly environments, both become weak and unable to escape the trap.

I call that trap sexual *bondage,* even though much of society today labels it sexual *addiction.* What's the difference? Virtually none. Both describe the condition of being under the control of sexual lust. However, I prefer the term bondage because it relates to the biblical concept of being a slave to sin, which is at the root of the problem. The apostle Paul referred to himself as a bond servant of Jesus Christ, and that's what all Christians are called to be. Whenever we allow anything or anyone to have a greater hold over our lives than Christ, we become a slave to it. We have elevated the power and authority of that person or thing over the power and authority of Christ in our lives, and that's sin.

I want to show in this book that, as bond-servants of Christ, we can and should have victory over sexual immorality and bondage to sex because Christ has defeated Satan and sin. Since we can do all things through Christ who strengthens us (Philippians 4:13), we can find freedom in Christ from sexual bondage. The recovery movement believes that the answer to sexual *addiction* is therapy and behavior modification. I contend that the answer to sexual *bondage* is repentance and faith. When we renounce what we have done as sin and choose to believe the truth, we will be set free.

The issue of losing control to sexual desires was clearly illustrated to me when the "free sex" movement was gaining momentum in America. I was asked to visit a Marriage and Family class in a local secular college and present the Christian perspective on the topic, which I'm sure few students really understood. The class was made up primarily of women with a few men also present.

One young man was clearly disinterested in my presentation. He pulled his desk away from the group and read the newspaper while I talked. Apparently he was listening, however, because he frequently interjected a vulgar noise in protest of my beliefs.

When I opened the floor for questions, one young woman asked, "What do Christians believe about masturbation?"

Before I could answer, the young man announced proudly so everyone could hear, "Well, I masturbate every day!"

There was an awkward silence as the other students anticipated my response to his challenge. "Congratulations!" I said at last. "But can you *stop* masturbating?"

The young man was silent for the rest of the discussion. When class was dismissed, he waited for the other students to leave. As he strolled by me, he taunted, "So why would I want to stop?"

"I didn't ask if you *wanted* to stop," I replied. "I asked if you *can* stop, because if you *can't*, what you think is freedom is really bondage."

That's the issue: freedom versus bondage. If you are involved in sexually impure thoughts or deeds—activities that are clearly in opposition to God's Word, stop. If you *can't* stop doing what you know you shouldn't do, then you, like Jon, are in bondage to those thought patterns and activities and need to find your freedom in Christ. This book was written to help you succeed where all your self-determination, willpower, and counseling appointments have fallen short.

Levels of Involvement

What is included in the broad category of sexual bondage? We can find some helpful answers in the work of those who study sexual addiction. Dr. Patrick Carnes, arguably the leading secular expert in the field of sexual addiction, has studied persons caught in the trap of compulsive sexual activity. In his book, *Contrary to Love,* he describes three descending developmental phases of sexual addiction.[1] An individual can be in bondage at one level without necessarily descending to the next. Each successive phase is characterized by increased relationship-avoidant behaviors.

Phase One: Normative Activity

The first level consists of behaviors that are generally considered normative in secular society, meaning that they are fairly common and accepted—though reluctantly by some—in our culture. These behaviors often employ exploitation and victimization—short of criminal violence—as a basis for greater sexual excitement. They include:

Sexual fantasy and masturbation. Our secular society generally views fantasy, whether or not it is accompanied by physical self-stimulation to orgasm, as an accepted and sometimes healthy diversion from the stresses of real life. Sexual fantasy is judged by many to be a harmless release of sexual energy because, technically speaking, a mental act won't violate anyone or constitute unfaithfulness to a spouse.

Thus, a man may see nothing wrong with fantasizing about having sex with a female coworker, a friend's wife, an erotic dancer in a nude bar, a seductive image on the video screen, etc. A woman may project herself into a romance novel and vicariously submit to the lovemaking of the handsome, flawless hero. Fantasizing is often accompanied by masturbation as the individual seeks the physical climax his or her fantasy partner cannot provide. But every fantasy becomes another link in a chain encircling the soul. Eventually such a person has difficulty interacting with others without being dominated by impure thoughts and desires.

Pornography. Anything which is intended to arouse sexual desire falls under the heading of pornography. Though some pornographic materials are still considered illegal, our society is inundated with expressions of pornography which, though perhaps offensive to some, are acceptable to many. Magazines offering "entertainment for men," such as *Playboy* and *Penthouse*, abound. Novels line the shelves of our bookstores and libraries which describe in graphic detail every possible perversion of God's design for sex.

Sexually explicit films rated R, NR-17, and X have migrated from the adult bookstore into the mall multiplex theaters as films for "mature audiences." Cable TV channels can be accessed which broadcast one sex act after another—homosexual as well as heterosexual—under the banner of "adult entertainment." And network television doesn't seem to be far behind.

Add to this list the sexually explicit lyrics in some popular music, live sex shows in many urban centers, 1-900 sex hot lines, and now even computer sex. The seemingly unquenchable demand in our culture for sexual stimulation is matched by a seemingly endless and varied supply. And most of it is legal and easily accessible.

Satan, the god of this world, has orchestrated the subtle erosion of moral standards in our nation. He has numbed the senses of this generation to sexually explicit material so we no longer react to it. A Christian who dabbles in pornography is like a soldier marching blindfolded through a mine field. Sooner or later poor judgment and careless experimentation will explode in his or her face.

Illicit affairs and/or prostitution. Premarital and extramarital sex seems to be widely accepted today (except perhaps by the individuals who are cheated on). Conversely, abstinence and marital fidelity are often viewed as outdated and prudish.

The media is doing a high-powered sell job on the issue. Movies and television sitcoms make light of adolescents losing their virginity and singles hopping from bed partner to bed partner. Characters who can't or won't "score" are often pictured as oddballs. Daytime dramas glamorize the violation of marriage vows and justify adultery in the name of "true love." Frequenting houses of prostitution or sexual massage parlors or bath houses to pay for sex is often treated comically. Furthermore, homosexual relationships are being pictured as a viable alternative lifestyle. The relentless theme is that consenting adults are free to follow their sexual urges apart from a commitment of marriage.

Christians who allow themselves to be influenced by the world's declining standards with regard to sexual activity are morally drifting downstream toward dangerous waters and an eventual waterfall. Every compromise leads to another, and a plunge into sexual bondage awaits them.

Phase Two: Indecent Activity

The second phase of sexual addiction finds the individual taking liberties which are considered indecent if not criminal by much of society. Persons involved in these types of activities often seek to intensify their sexual pleasure by performing for an audience—usually an *unwilling* audience. These people may already be in bondage to one or more activities in phase one. But like a drug addict seeking a higher high, they seek greater risk in order to secure a greater sexual thrill.

Behaviors in this category include exhibitionism (also known as indecent exposure, displaying genitals in public, flashing, or streaking), voyeurism (sexual arousal through viewing sexual objects or activity, "peeping toms"), transvestism (cross-dressing), bestiality (sex with animals), obscene letters or phone calls, fetishism (sexual arousal from objects such as clothing), necrophilia (sex with corpses), and a variety of indecent public acts.

Phase Three: Extreme Activity

Persons at this level violate their victims with painful and criminal acts. The nature of these acts is generally considered so vile that the perpetrators are often viewed as subhuman and incorrigible. This is the level where we find sociopathic sex criminals such as serial murderers Ted Bundy and Jeffrey Dahmer. Behaviors at this level include child molestation, incest, rape, and sadomasochism (giving and receiving pain to heighten sexual pleasure).

According to Dr. Carnes, not everyone progresses automatically from one phase to the next. Rather, the phases are a means of categorizing sexual addiction according to the degree of personal risk involved. He notes, however, that a person's sexual behavior seldom remains frozen at one level but includes a wide range of expressions drawn from other tiers. Thus someone who victimizes others with indecent exposure may also be in bondage to pornography and involved in an illicit relationship.

It may seem unthinkable to you that someone who is "innocently" hooked on *Playboy* or peep shows could descend to the depths of a serial sex criminal and murderer. But don't underestimate the power of the kingdom of darkness when a doorway is willingly and persistently opened to it. The only safe recourse is to slam that door shut and return to the light of moral purity as presented in God's Word.

You Can Be Free!

You may have picked up this book because you have a problem with nagging sexual temptations or defeating bad habits in this area. For example, perhaps you have trouble staying away from sexy reading material. You once rationalized that *Playboy* magazine, the lingerie catalogs your wife receives in the mail, or novels with explicit sex scenes were harmless entertainment as long as you didn't act out the temptations and fantasies that filled your mind. But now you're aware that you have flown far past the browsing stage. You know where to get the materials you want without being recognized. You throw away your stash from time to time, but in a few days or weeks you're back for more. You're hooked on the stuff, and you find yourself craving even more risque pictures and stories.

Maybe your biggest problem is with obscene movies and videos. You tell yourself that you watch them for the story while trying to ignore the steamy sex scenes. After all, a lot of Christians attend movies featuring sex, violence, and nudity without consequences—or so it seems. But not so with you. You can't get enough of the erotic scenes which are steadily lining the walls of your mind with posters that feed your sexual fantasies.

Perhaps you have jokingly told your friends that you are a soap opera and romance novel junkie. But deep inside you know it's no joke. You plan your day around the afternoon soaps, and the Bible on your nightstand has been buried under a stack of trashy books for months. You don't want to be dependent on that stuff for a sexual and emotional buzz, but you can't seem to help it.

Or maybe you are secretly trapped in another unscriptural sexual behavior: an extramarital sexual relationship; an insistent fascination and attraction to homosexuality; or tendencies toward exhibitionism or sadomasochism. You know that what you're doing is wrong. You wish you could retrace every misstep that got you into this mess in the first place. And you realize that every act drives you deeper into the darkness of your bondage.

But try as you might, you can't stop—and you don't know what to do about it. You long to be free, but you're afraid that you are headed down the same dark, dead-end street that caused Jon and Angela, at the beginning of this chapter, so much pain and heartache.

If you really want to be free from your sexual bondages, I have good news for you. You can be free! Jon, who is an acquaintance of my colleague in ministry, Russ Rummer, is living proof. You will be interested to hear the rest of his story.

When Angela told Jon to leave their home, it drove him to the breaking point. He went to the mountains with some friends to pick up the pieces. One of Jon's friends gave him my book, *The Bondage Breaker*, and he devoured it. He learned about the origin of the sexual strongholds which had ruled his life for so many years. Then in one three-hour session with God, Jon followed the Steps to Freedom found in *The Bondage Breaker* and in Appendix A of this book. He renounced the strongholds in his life and dealt with a number of issues which had contributed to his bondage. Jon later told Russ, "It was the most freeing time I have ever spent with God."

Then Jon got involved in a small group of others who had been set free from various bondages. Jon states, "God began a process of rebuilding me from the ground up. It appeared that He wanted me to learn something clearly. I had to be real about the pain I had caused my wife and how broken I felt about being kicked out of our marriage."

For the next couple of months God put Jon through a kind of spiritual boot camp. Through the support and prayers of his friends, his group, and Russ Rummer, God began to renew Jon's relationship with Angela. During this time she also went through the Steps to Freedom and began attending the support group with Jon. After three months of separation, Jon and Angela were reunited. Today Jon is free from his sexual bondages, and his marriage is growing stronger.

Jon concludes, "My job still takes me on the road a lot, but things are different. Angela and I support each other during this time. When I check into my hotel room, I get down on my knees and pray for strength. Then I expose all the hiding places in the room and get rid of any pornography I find, and I use a block-out code on the TV to keep the trashy movies out of my room. When I feel particularly tempted, I call Angela and have her pray with me."

Jon admits that he isn't perfect; he has slipped a few times. But he no longer cycles through the guilt, anger, and remorse that used to dominate his thinking. When the temptations come, he now knows what to do about them. His greatest relief is that he doesn't have to hide anymore. Jon is free!

This book was written to help you find your freedom from whatever sexual bondages are robbing you of your victory in Christ and hindering your maturity in Christ. (Or if you're reading so you can assist others find their freedom in Christ, this book will be a great help to you as well.) There are no magic formulas to follow. Rather, the information in this book will reacquaint you with the truth of God's Word regarding sexual temptation, sexual bondage, Satan's destructive role in the struggle, your identity in Christ, and God's provision for your freedom. Also, the Steps to Freedom in Christ in Appendix A will guide you in renouncing behaviors which have kept you bound and in appropriating the freedom which is your inheritance in Christ.

It is important that you understand not only the freedom Christ has provided for you but how you got into bondage in the first place. Part One of this book identifies the pathways to sexual bondage, traces these pathways back to Adam and Eve in the Garden of Eden, exposes

Satan's insidious lies about sex, outlines God's design for sex and marriage, and explores the negative consequences from ignoring that design.

Part Two centers on the way of escape from sexual temptation and bondage which Jesus Christ has provided for us. You will learn what you need to *believe* and what you need to *do* to secure your freedom in Christ. You will discover how to win the battle for your mind over sexual temptation. And you will be encouraged to begin your recovery in Christ and walk free of the sinful strongholds blocking your joy and growth in Christ.

This book is also for those who have been sexually exploited by others through rape, incest, molestation, etc. Most of the people who come to Freedom in Christ Ministries for help can trace their problems to some kind of sexual abuse. I want to show how the gospel will put an end to victimization and stop the cycle of abuse. I believe that Christ is the only answer, and that the truth can set both the victim and the perpetrator free.

As I worked on this book, it has been my prayer that you will find the sexual freedom that Jesus Christ purchased for you on the cross. No matter how you got into the shackles of sexual sin that now hobble you, there is freedom for you if you will throw yourself upon the mercy of God. Freedom comes through "Christ in you, the hope of glory" (Colossians 1:27). Jesus Christ is the bondage breaker. He is the way of escape.

The Lure of a Sex-Crazed World

Elaine, a Christian woman, divorced her adulterous husband ten years ago. As a single mother with one child, she had done her best to provide for herself and be a good parent. But she struggled with loneliness and craved meaningful social interaction which her church wasn't providing.

I first met Elaine at a meeting of Parents without Partners. As a seminary professor, I had been asked to speak to the group on the topic of parenting. My presentation was sandwiched between happy hour and the dance! Elaine had a cigarette in one hand and an alcoholic drink in the other. As I watched her, it was obvious that she neither smoked nor drank, for the cigarette burned to ashes in the ash tray and the ice cubes melted in her untouched drink. She just wanted to fit into the group.

The next time I saw Elaine was in my office a few months later. She was in tears. Her overwhelming need for companionship and acceptance and the pressure of the worldly crowd had led her to compromise her moral convictions. A one-night stand with her boss had left her pregnant. "Why did God do this to me?" she sobbed.

I wanted to say, "Lady, God didn't shove you into that bed." But instead I felt compassion for her and frustrated that some of our churches are unable to meet the needs of people like Elaine, turning them out into a world that glitters with temptations which lure people into immorality.

Is it any wonder that sexual bondage is a major problem in our nation, considering the moral nosedive we are in? We couldn't be more hospitable to the influences of the world, the flesh, and the devil in the area of sexual immorality if we posted a sign at every border inviting, "Come on in and take over—we're open to anything."

For example, the evening news recently captured the anguished outcry of a woman in an upper-middle-class suburb. Thrusting a pamphlet toward the camera, she proclaimed, "This kind of literature cannot come into our schools!" We would understand her concern if the pamphlet promoted sexual license, homosexuality, or abortion. But the material was a clear, well-documented argument in favor of sexual abstinence before marriage. Although it was published by *Focus on the Family,* the pamphlet contained no reference to God and no mention of Scripture. But she was still against the promotion of abstinence among today's youth by a Christian organization. I couldn't help but wonder what she was teaching her children. Most Americans only a generation ago were incensed at the idea of promoting premarital sex, condoning homosexuality, and offering free condoms in our schools.

Sexual promiscuity is rampant today, and many consider unrealistic the expectation that our young people will abstain from sex until marriage. But have we given up on our kids too easily? Interviewing several honor students from mainland China, CBS news anchor Connie Chung asked if Chinese youth engaged in sex before marriage. "That would be wrong!" they responded.

"Do you mean to tell me that none of you have had premarital sex?" Chung pressed. The students shook their heads and again expressed their conviction that sex before marriage is wrong. What is deemed an unrealistic expectation in a "Christian" nation is a socially accepted norm in a country where Christianity is officially suppressed! In each case the youth are living up to the expectations of their respective societies. We simply expect too little from our kids. In reality, we can't impose a morality on them that we refuse to impose on ourselves.

Are we a Christian nation? Hardly! More pornographic filth is produced in America than in any other nation of the world. For example, the majority of all child pornography comes out of the Los Angeles area, where Freedom In Christ Ministries is headquartered.

Within the dark realm of pornography, nothing has greater potential to undo America than uncensored cable television coming into our homes. There was a time when a person had to attend a public adult theater to view hardcore pornography. This "inconvenience" kept many people from getting involved, fearing that their reputations would be lost if they were seen going into these sleaze parlors.

But with the proliferation of VCR's and the cable and satellite networks, any home can become a sleaze parlor with the customers veiled in virtual anonymity—only the TV company knows who has signed up for the porn channels. Furthermore, almost every hotel provides in-room "adult entertainment" via satellite or cable, with the viewing guests cloaked in privacy.

Even network television is influenced by our nation's loose morals. My colleague, Russ Rummer, recently shared with me his evaluation of an evening of TV programming.

A few nights ago while I was exercising my male prerogative with the remote control, I flipped between two popular TV sitcoms. In a span of three to four minutes I was shocked by two separate, overtly sexual segments.

One involved the lead female character being asked to spend the night with a man she had just met—and she agreed. It was as casual and matter-of-fact as if they had decided to have lunch together. But the next scene really struck me. The character's sister was seated on the couch telling a friend about her sister's impending sexual escapade. She said she hoped her sister didn't hurt the man, because she hadn't had sex in a long time. The line got a big laugh from the studio audience.

The other program dramatized various expressions of the young male character's raging hormones. In one scene he was giving kissing lessons to a girl his age. When I flipped back a few minutes later, he walked through the door and sat down on the couch next to his dog. He commented that he bet his supposedly sexually inactive dog wished he could be like him—an accomplished sex athlete. A voice dubbed in for the dog said, "No, I don't. I've already had sex." And that line got a huge laugh.

The vast majority of all references to sex on television or in movies pertain to sex outside of marriage. Seldom are the negative consequences of immoral behavior shown. James Bond never contracts a sexually transmitted disease, and we rarely see the damaging emotional effects of one-night stands on future relationships.

Living in a World of Sexual Myths

A major reason for our nation's preoccupation with sex in general and sexual immorality in particular is the myths about sex which dominate our society. Although these myths are contrary to the teaching of Scripture, many Christians are swept up in them because the expression of them pervades the media, as exemplified by Russ's night of TV viewing just mentioned. Perhaps your struggle with sexual temptation and sin is the result of being deceived into believing one or more of the following myths as truth.

Sexual fulfillment is the ultimate panacea for personal happiness. This myth permeates our society's music, movies, television sitcoms, dramas, soaps, and advertising. The message pounds at us like a frenzied drumbeat: Life will be perfect if all your sexual drives, needs, and wants are met. Don't let anything stand in the way of getting what you want, not the "old-fashioned" values of abstinence and marital fidelity, and especially not archaic biblical morality.

The mythical happy ending always seems to include the hero coaxing the girl into bed—or vice versa. Sexual conquest is the game, and we apparently have the right to get our share no matter who we use or how we use them to do it. And Madison Avenue suggests that this new car, that brand of toothpaste, this exotic fragrance, or that line of clothes will help us get what we want just like they do in the movies.

It must be horrible to have someone "love" you for his or her own personal sexual gratification. It must be heartbreaking to wake up and realize that all he or she wanted was your body. How many people are being used this way in the name of love? All that is developed is lust, and all that is fed is the ego. No meaningful relationship is established, nor is any legitimate need being met. How degrading! It seems to be the great ambition of man to be happy as animals instead of being blessed as children of God.

The world's concept of happiness is having what we want. God's concept of happiness is wanting what we have (1 Thessalonians 5:18; 1 Timothy 6:6-8), which includes the sexual area of our lives. What we have are God's guidelines for moral purity in the Bible, His blessings as we live within those guidelines, and freedom in Christ if we get entangled in sexual bondage. If you really want to be happy, ignore the myth that sexual license is the key. Learn to be thankful for what you have, not greedy for what you don't have.

Sex is the way to catch and keep the person you love, especially for women. According to this myth, everybody wants sex. If you aren't a willing and satisfying sex partner, you may lose the person you want and look like a prude in the process. So even if you don't feel like it or have qualms of conscience against it, you had better perform or you will lose out.

Enlightening research related to this myth was conducted by sociologist Wendy Luttrell of Duke University and health educator Peter Anderson of the University of New Orleans and presented to the Society for the Scientific Study of Sex.[1] Anderson's survey of 489 students showed that about one in five women and one in three men "drink more than normal to make it easier to have sex." Luttrell reported on 13 student-designed surveys of 3003 Duke University students over seven years. Although findings vary from year to year, there are key patterns:

• About 40 percent of the students, both male and female, use drugs to affect their sexual behavior and say it changes their willingness to make love.

• Between 20 percent and 40 percent of the women say they have been physically or verbally coerced into sex; 3 percent of the men report that they have been coerced.

• More than 50 percent of the women have pretended to enjoy sex when they didn't, versus fewer than 10 percent of the men.

• Between 30 percent and 85 percent of the women—depending on the survey—say they have changed their minds during the sex act, deciding they didn't want to participate; 5 percent to 20 percent of the men report it has happened to them.

Diane Sawyer reported on "Prime Time Live" that 33 percent of American girls have had sexual intercourse by the end of the ninth grade and 70 percent by the end of high school. She interviewed several sexually active teenage girls, some as young as eighth graders, who claimed to have had as many as ten different partners. At the end of the segment, Sawyer reported, "Every single one of these sexually active girls confided with us that they wish they'd said no."[2]

Does a woman or man have to perform sexually to be accepted and loved? No, that's a demeaning myth leading to sexual bondage.

Whatever two consenting adults do behind closed doors doesn't hurt anyone else. That's a lie. Those consenting adults are someone's son, daughter, brother, sister, mother, or father. Think of the shame and hurt these people may suffer as a result of their loved ones' consensual but immoral behavior. Also, the private liaison may result in a pregnancy leading to an abortion or an unwanted and abused child. That's serious hurt. And a sexually transmitted disease will surely affect the friends and family members of the persons infected.

Furthermore, God was in the bedroom with those two consenting adults. Secret sin on earth is open scandal in heaven. What we choose to do or not do before God affects all humanity and eventually impacts eternity.

Activities that should be forbidden to children are all right for "adults only." This myth asserts that a child's mind will be polluted from seeing nudity in magazines or watching sex scenes on a cable channel, but an adult's won't. That's another lie. When did God establish a different standard of morality for children than for adults? He didn't. If something is morally wrong for your child, then it is morally wrong for you. You will never be so mature that pornography will not be harmful to you.

You cannot legislate morality. Nonsense! Of course we can legislate morality. That's what our elected lawmakers do all the time. If they couldn't legislate morality, we wouldn't have any laws against murder, rape, theft, etc. Every bill passed by the legislature is based on someone's concept of morality. What the secularists are saying is that Christians have no business imposing *biblical* morality on a secular society. They insist that the separation of church and state guarantees that government and due process of law are free from the intrusion of the church and its moral standards.

But that's not what the First Amendment is about. It guarantees that the government cannot interfere with the establishment and free exercise of religion. The First Amendment says nothing about the separation of church and state, nor does it forbid the influence of biblical morality upon our laws. Indeed, when the Constitution was framed it was anchored to the bedrock of the Word of God. But our nation has slipped off its foundation to the shifting sands of popular opinion regarding righteousness and morality.

Our country is paying a high price for accepting these myths about sex as truth and ignoring the moral decline these lies encourage. The epidemic of HIV and other sexually transmitted diseases, a generation of babies sacrificed to convenience abortions, the breakdown of the nuclear family through adultery, abandonment, and divorce, and the rise of sexual abuse and sex crimes are glaring examples.

"But what about the Christian community?" you may ask. "We're not being overrun by the HIV epidemic. We're not flocking to the abortion clinics. We listen to Dr. James Dobson on the radio and value the family. Is the declining moral climate really affecting us?"

Most definitely, though perhaps not as obviously. It may appear that our values as Christian people have restrained us from following the world into immorality at the same breakneck pace. But our experience at Freedom In Christ Ministries has convinced us that believers are no less affected by the relentless, manifold temptations to sexual sin which permeate our culture. It's just that most Christians who get sucked into this trap, like Jon in the previous chapter, keep it a secret from their brothers and sisters in Christ in order to maintain an appearance of holiness.

So instead of openly engaging in an extramarital affair or homosexual relationship, they secretly toy with pornography, sexual fantasies, voyeurism, or whatever while trying to serve Christ. And they come to us by the defeated hundreds complaining of a lack of spiritual fervor, a nonexistent devotional life with Christ, marriages on the brink of collapse, and substance abuse addictions. And without exception, everyone we have counseled who was in bondage in some other way was also in sexual bondage at some level. Happily, when these people take responsibility for their bondages and take the Steps to Freedom in Christ, they are set free.

How do so many Christians get pulled into this quagmire? I see three major pathways to sexual bondage which are graded and paved by our culture's preoccupation with self and sex. In the next chapter I will describe these three pathways to help you identify how you found the dark detour into sexual bondage.

T H R E E

Pathways to Sexual Bondage

No one purposely sets out to become trapped in sexual bondage. First, a person is tempted to fulfill legitimate sexual needs in the world, the flesh, or the devil instead of in Christ. Each temptation brings him to the threshold of a decision. If he hesitates at the threshold instead of immediately taking the thought "captive to the obedience of Christ" (2 Corinthians 10:5 NASB), he increases his chances of yielding to that temptation.

Next, if he continues to yield to sexual temptation, he will form a habit. And if he exercises that habit long enough, a stronghold will be established in his mind. Once a stronghold of thought and response is entrenched in the mind, it is extremely difficult to act contrary to that pattern. Sexual bondage is a stronghold in the mind which causes the individual to act contrary to the will of God, even when he or she knows and desires otherwise.

In order to be set free from the sexual bondage which grips you, you must understand how you got involved in the first place. You must identify the pathway which drew you into sexual bondage so you can renounce those impure thoughts and behaviors. And you must identify any persons who may have aided or encouraged you in this wrong direction so you may forgive them.

In the process of teaching and counseling on this topic, I have discovered three broad pathways which lead to sexual bondage. The first pathway is *sexual promiscuity*—participating in activities that encourage lust and illicit sex: pornography, fantasy, voyeurism, sexual experimentation, etc. The second pathway is *sexual disorientation*—fascination with or exposure to homosexual influences. The third pathway is *sexual abuse*—hurtful experiences and negative influences from the past which predispose an individual to impurity. In this chapter we will examine these three pathways and identify how they lead the careless or unwitting victim into bondage.

It must be noted that few people find these pathways alone. The people in our past and present—parents, grandparents, siblings, other relatives, family friends, peers, coworkers—exert tremendous influence in our lives. Sometimes these individuals give us an intentional or unintentional push in the wrong direction. For example, a boy is introduced to pornography by his father, who carelessly leaves smutty magazines and videos where the boy can find them. A bachelor neighbor befriends an unpopular teenage boy and influences him into homosexuality. A little girl is molested by her uncle for years and grows up to be a sexually promiscuous teenager, or she shuts down sexually and cannot seem to enjoy a legitimate sexual relationship with her husband.

You may have been forced onto the pathway to sexual bondage when you were too young to understand or object. You may have been encouraged into immoral behavior by someone you trusted before you knew the act was immoral. "I'm hooked, and it's not my fault," you contend.

It may be true that you are not fully responsible for the sin you got into. But you *are* responsible for choosing to remain there. As you explore the reasons behind your bondage, be encouraged that Jesus Christ has provided a way of escape. However, you can't blame anyone but yourself if you aren't free; you must take the exit God has provided. Part Two and Appendix A of this book will help you do so.

Playing with Fire

Andy came into sexual bondage by following the pathway of sexual promiscuity. He grew up in a church-going family in the South. As a young boy he learned about pornography from his older brothers, who hid the magazines from their parents but not from him. All through Christian elementary school and high school, Andy's secret fascination with pornography intensified. The books and magazines he collected were increasingly more graphic and lewd. He restrained from physical sex because it was clearly a sin, but sexual fantasies consumed his waking thoughts.

By the time Andy entered a Christian university in a southwestern state, printed pornography no longer satisfied his ravenous appetite for sexual excitement. He began sneaking off to adult theaters and nude bars. He rented and viewed X-rated videos. He searched out live sex shows in the sleaziest parts of town. Yet he would not participate in sex, either in the dark dives he visited or with the available coeds at the university. Instead, he continued to be a model student and married a beautiful girl, Trish.

Moving to another part of the country to begin his career, Andy's sexual bondage held him like a vise. He quickly located and frequently patronized the porno attractions in the city without Trish's knowledge. His job permitted him time to rent videos and take them home while his wife was at work. As a 25-year-old, Andy lamented, "I'm a Christian, and I have never been unfaithful to Trish. But I have done almost everything a man can do without having illicit sex, and I have poured thousands of dollars into my disgusting 'habit.' I'm a sexual addict, and I don't know how to get free."

Andy's pathway to bondage was sexual promiscuity. Although he did not have intercourse with anyone other than Trish for fear of disgracing his family or contracting HIV, he admits that he has consistently violated Christ's instruction in Matthew 5:27,28: "You have heard that it was said, 'Do not commit adultery.' But I tell you that anyone who looks at a woman lustfully has already committed adultery with her in his heart." Andy has been sexually promiscuous with countless numbers of women in every way except physically. And it all began with the dirty magazines which captivated him as a child.

Sexual promiscuity is a major pathway to sexual bondage. I have heard variations of Andy's story from scores of men: pornographic magazines and movies leading to sexual fantasies, uncontrolled masturbation, and voyeurism leading to experimentation, adultery, prostitution, or worse. I hear similar accounts from women about being sucked into fantasy and unfaithfulness through their involvement with romance novels and dramas. People who play with fire by dabbling in impure sexual thoughts and activities invite a fire storm of sexual bondage.

Desperate for freedom from his bondage, Andy finally admitted his problem to Trish. The couple attended sexual addiction therapy sessions together for two years with little success. Recently, the women's Bible study group Trish belonged to at their church studied *Victory over the Darkness* and *The Bondage Breaker*, and she was filled with hope. At her encouragement, Andy read the two books and met with two men from the church who walked him through the Steps to Freedom in Christ. Andy is finally on the path to freedom from the pornography and mental promiscuity which had bound him.

The Lie of the "Alternate Lifestyle"

Thomas unintentionally discovered another pathway to sexual bondage: homosexuality. He was raised by a domineering mother and a detached father he could never seem to please. Possessing a brilliant mind, Thomas found his acceptance in academics, graduating from college with a teaching degree. He also found great happiness with Claudia, whom he married, and their shared faith in Christ. Together they moved to a large city where Thomas began his career as associate professor of history at a small private college.

Thomas's life was full and satisfying. Claudia's love and acceptance warmed him. His teaching position provided many opportunities for stimulating academic growth. He taught an adult Sunday school class at the church they attended. They were blessed by the birth of a daughter and, 14 months later, a son.

But the responsibility of parenthood brought unexpected pressures and conflict to Thomas's marriage, activating old memories of his mother's dominance and his father's displeasure. The stress at home drove him deeper into his academic pursuits. He spent increasing amounts of time away from Claudia doing research for articles submitted to various professional publications. His relationship with God began to wane as he buried himself in his work.

That's when Thomas got involved with Aaron, a history department colleague whom he had once attempted to lead to Christ. As their friendship deepened, Aaron admitted to Thomas his years of inner turmoil over his sexual orientation. Thomas determined to guide his friend out of his delusion to the truth of God's Word.

Thomas accompanied Aaron into the seedy world of the gay bar scene, rationalizing his behavior as research for helping his friend. But instead of pulling his friend out, Thomas was pulled in. The homosexual lifestyle was seductively fascinating to him. He was awakened to memories of boyhood experiences which had caused him to doubt his own sexual identity. Thomas remembered his father being more accepting of a younger brother, who was involved in athletics and deemed more masculine than the academically inclined Thomas. He recalled his father shaming him for crying over the loss of his pet guinea pig, saying, "Only little girls cry about such a thing."

In time, Thomas yielded to his first sexual encounter with a man. He felt compelled to seek "freedom to be himself." He found himself justifying his quest for personal sexual pleasure to compensate for the love he missed out on as a child. He felt wonderfully loved and validated by the homosexual community, which seemed far more accepting than the people in his church. So he became more deeply involved in homosexual affairs, but he kept his exploits a secret, leading a double life.

Yet a conflict raged within Thomas. On one hand, he believed—though his belief was based on deception—that God had created him to be a homosexual. What else would explain his inner turmoil over his father's disapproval and his conflicts with Claudia? What else could account for the satisfaction and acceptance he experienced among other homosexual men? On the other hand, he could not escape his understanding of God's Word on the subject of sexual purity. He felt convicted about being unfaithful to Claudia. He feared the consequences reaped by those who seek fulfillment in fleshly behaviors—and homosexuality was at the top of the list. Thomas was terribly confused about his relationship with God and how to balance his desire to be a Christian with his awareness of being a homosexual.

No longer willing to continue the charade at home, Thomas left Claudia and moved in with a homosexual friend. He began attending a gay church but was repulsed by the attempt to blend Christianity and the homosexual lifestyle. Gay pride and gay rights were emphasized and worshiped more than God. Sex play in the pews during services was condoned. Thomas felt caught between two opposing forces. Continuing to believe that he was created to be homosexual clashed with everything he knew about God and faith. But he didn't know how to extract himself from the punishing dilemma.

Thomas was in bondage to the lie that homosexuality is a viable alternative to God's design for human sexuality. Like so many people involved in homosexuality, he became trapped after repeated steps down a pathway of fascination with homosexuality, prompted by hurtful childhood experiences and clouded logic leading to poor choices as an adult.

"But it wasn't his fault," some may argue. "Thomas came from a dysfunctional family. His father and mother provided a skewed picture of male and female roles. His poor self-identity and subsequent behavior is the product of his environment."

As mentioned earlier, other people may be partially or substantially responsible for setting us on the pathway to sexual bondage. And Satan takes advantage of these failures to establish strongholds of control in the lives of misused or abused children and youth. These people and experiences must be dealt with in the process of finding our freedom in Christ from Satan's bondage. However, the focus at this point should not be on who is to blame but on finding the way of escape. On that count the individual in bondage is fully responsible to take those important steps.

The Violation of the Innocent

A third pathway to sexual bondage is the experience of being the victim of another person's illicit sexual exploits. Some of these people were molested as children by trusted adults. Some were the victims of incest by a parent or sibling. Some were date-raped as teens or violently raped as adults. Some were the victims of ritual sex abuse by members of a cult. The common thread among these victims is that they were sexually violated against their will. And the traumatic acts perpetrated by others on many of these innocent victims opened the door to their own sexual bondage.

Not all victims of sexual abuse end up in sexual bondage. But a surprising number of the people we counsel at Freedom In Christ Ministries admit that they have been sexually abused in some way.

As with many victims, Melissa's memories of sexual abuse were blocked by the trauma she experienced. At one point, had you asked her if she had been abused as a child, she would have said no. But her poor self-image and strange behavior as a child signaled a deep, hidden problem. Melissa told her story to my colleague Russ:

> I felt so inadequate and unacceptable as a child. I avoided getting close to anyone, especially boys, fearing they would find out how terrible I was. Everyone seemed to react to me in a sexual way. As a girl of six or seven, men whispered to me what they wanted to do to me when I got older. As I grew up, women seemed threatened by me, as if I intended to steal their husbands. This behavior only reinforced my belief that there was something wrong with me, and everyone saw it. I had become a Christian as a young child, but I was convinced that God had picked me out to be sexually tormented and abused.
>
> About the time I turned nine or ten, I began to experiment with masturbation. I also became quite self-destructive. I cut the insides of my legs and put alcohol on the wounds to make them hurt more. I cut pieces of skin off my knuckles just to feel the pain I knew I deserved. As a young teen I was shy and afraid of boys. I didn't have many friends. When I dated, I either froze up after a little bit of necking or blanked out, unable to remember what I did or how I got home. I became bulimic at about 14.
>
> I rededicated my life to Christ at age 15. But as I left high school and entered college I continued to binge and purge once or twice a day. I also strayed

into a few sexual involvements, and most of those guys were also Christians. I wanted to be loved and accepted, so I gave them my body. But when I did, the boys just used me and discarded me. With or without sex, the boys rejected me. I felt dirty and trapped.

When Melissa married Dan in her early twenties, their physical intimacy opened a floodgate of memories and nightmares about her clouded past. She dreamed about her grandfather raping her while her new husband watched with enjoyment. Gradually the repressed memories of her horrifying past came into focus.

Melissa remembered being molested by her grandfather at age two. She was forced to accept and perform oral sex and other atrocities with him as a young child. At the time she was cutting herself, she also awakened often in the middle of the night with severe abdominal pains. An insightful doctor told Melissa's mother that she was being sexually abused. The mother blamed Melissa's stepfather, brother, and uncle—everyone but her grandfather, the man who was doing it.

Melissa felt betrayed by the doctor for revealing her "secret." She had never considered telling anyone how Grandpa "loved" her, even though she felt it was wrong. She was confused. She loved her grandfather, but she also prayed that God would kill him to make the abuse stop. And when he *did* die before Melissa became a teenager, she felt responsible and mourned him. But the inner wounds he had inflicted continued to torment her for years.

Sexual abuse is a broad pathway to all kinds of bondage, including sexual bondage. Studies show that nearly half of all female children will experience some form of sexual abuse before they reach their fourteenth birthday.[1] Furthermore, the perpetrators of 85 to 94 percent of sexual violations are either relatives, family friends, neighbors, or acquaintances of the victim, not strangers.[2]

Traumatic betrayal at such an impressionable age prompts distorted thinking in many victims of sexual abuse. Instead of blaming the perpetrator, who may be a relative she desperately wants to trust and love, a girl blames God for not protecting her. Others feel emotionally cut off from God, saying, "I know God loves me, but my heart is numb to my relationship with Him, because He all but violated me Himself by letting it happen."

The victim may also mistakenly blame herself for allowing such a thing to happen. As with Melissa, the thinking of abuse victims may center on self-blame and poor self-image leading to self-loathing and self-destructive behavior for "allowing" the abuse to occur. Victims of rape often become their own victimizers as a result of intense feelings of shock, denial, fear, guilt, depression, and disorientation. These feelings may lead to disorganization, suicide attempts, phobic avoidance of the opposite sex, and nightmarish dreams.[3]

Many young victims of sexual abuse, like Melissa, unconsciously protect themselves by blocking out the memories of these sad events. The intensity of the trauma overloads their young minds and pushes those memories into a dark corner. This defense against the pain works well for children, but as they grow older it hampers their hold on reality. Many begin acting out their excessive need for love and protection and find those needs satisfied by sex. This is why many who are caught in the web of sexual bondage cannot explain how they ended up there

Melissa's pain didn't end with the realization of her grandfather's abuse. Unfortunately, her Christian husband Dan was in bondage to pornography and alcohol, and he sometimes subjected her to sexual acts against her will. But when Melissa pressed for a divorce after three years of marriage, Dan found help with a counselor who led him through the Steps to Freedom in Christ. Melissa did the same, confessing the hurt, anger, and confusion that attended her history of sexual abuse. Their lives and marriage were so radically changed that it's hard to believe they are the same persons.

Melissa now understands how much God loves her and realizes that her grandfather's sins can no longer touch her. She is free to enjoy life with the man who loves and accepts her completely. Her complete restoration from the bondage caused by sexual abuse is still in process as she walks in the truth of her freedom from the traumas of her childhood and adult years. The same victory is available to all of God's children who desire release from bondage.

Perhaps while reading this chapter you have recognized a pathway which has led you into the sexually impure thought patterns and behaviors which now seem to control you. And you have possibly identified thoughts, events, and persons which have ushered you down this path to bondage. As important as these discoveries may be, you yet need to get to the core of your sexual bondage. This issue is the subject of Chapter 4.

The Pimp
in Your Mind

There is more behind sexual bondage than the sinking moral standards of our culture and the specific events or persons who were instrumental in ushering you down that path. The following story illustrates the point.

Before he met Christ, Rick's life was an endless quest for intimacy. As a child, he was sexually abused by his grandmother. After his father committed suicide, his mother became increasingly involved in religious activities, devoting her life to ministry. So as a young man Rick embarked on a desperate search to fill the hole which the sins of others had left in him. Even after his marriage to Emily, his college sweetheart, he kept trying to cover his bitterness and hurt with other sexual encounters, work, and the approval of others, but without success. Emily lost patience and left him.

One day while listening to a tape by Dr. Charles Stanley, Rick fell to his knees and asked Jesus to save him from himself and from the sin that never delivered what it promised. He and Emily were reconciled and eventually had four children. They seemed to be the model Christian family.

But deep inside, Rick was still taunted by the lie that sex, food, work, and other people could meet his needs more fully than Christ. He began listening to that lie and fell back into his old patterns of immorality. He became sexually involved with numerous partners, including a married woman, while continuing to play the role of the Christian husband and father. He lived a double life in constant turmoil.

Devastated at the breakup of an affair, Rick confessed everything to his family and entered a 12-step program for his addictions. Emily was crushed and told him not to return home. Then she divorced him.

Rick made an attempt at renewing his faith in Christ. He prayed and committed himself not to get involved in illicit sex for the 90 days of his treatment. But he failed, deceived into thinking that the right woman would meet his deep and seemingly unquenchable need for love. He got involved with another married woman while continuing to have daily devotions, seek God's guidance for his life, and witness to his coworkers.

For years Rick rode a spiritual and emotional roller coaster. Conviction would drive him to break off his relationships and return to the Lord. Then depression or problems would hit, and he would find himself seeking the same familiar ways of escape: illicit sex, food, success. He felt powerless to control his behavior. Rick recalls:

> The "pimp" in my mind repeatedly promised me fulfillment if I would only prostitute myself one more time. But he never fulfilled his promise. Life for me was like pushing a car. When things were going all

> right, it required only a little effort. But
> every time I tried to push the car over the
> mountain of my sexual bondage, the car
> rolled back over me, leaving me desperate,
> hurt, and without hope again. I couldn't stop
> this cycle no matter how much I sought God.
> My sexual addiction ruled everything in my
> life. I hated it, I knew it was destroying me
> from the inside out—but I kept heeding the
> pimp in my mind again and again.

Rick's mother invited him to attend my conference on
resolving personal and spiritual conflicts. He consented
to go, but during the first evening of the conference he
was harassed by sexual fantasies prompted by Satan, the
pimp in his mind. However, one statement did penetrate
and give him hope: "If the Son sets you free, you will be
free indeed" (John 8:36). Rick says, "I knew I wasn't
free. I was powerless to stop the fruitless search for fulfillment and satisfaction in sex, food, and work."

Rick's mother set up an appointment for Rick and me
to meet privately during the conference. He continues his
story:

> I knew while driving to the meeting that
> something was going to happen. My heart
> felt like it was going to explode. There was a
> war raging within me. The old pimp who had
> controlled my life for years didn't want me to
> go. But I was determined to experience the
> freedom Neil had talked about.
>
> I expected Neil to slap me on the side of
> the head and shout out an exorcistic prayer.

Then I would surely fall to the floor and flap around uncontrollably until the effects of his prayer set me free. But it didn't happen that way. Neil listened quietly as I shared my story, then he said in a calm voice, "Rick, I believe you can be free in Christ."

As Neil led me through the Steps to Freedom in Christ, I could hear the pimp's insistent lies in my mind. The inner battle was intense, but I was ready for the shackles to be broken. So I repented of my sin, renounced all the lies I had believed, renounced every sexual use of my body as an instrument of unrighteousness, and forgave all those who had offended me. As I did, peace began to roll in and drown out 37 years worth of lies. I heard holy silence. The pimp was gone and, praise God, I was free.

Rick's freedom was tested right away. The next day during the conference he was bombarded by immoral thoughts. But he stood firm in the power of the blood of Christ to resist them. That night he was strongly tempted to pursue another destructive relationship. But the moment he called on Christ's all-powerful, cleansing blood, the holy silence returned.

Since that conference, Rick has experienced a genuine and growing relationship with his heavenly Father. He has stopped watching TV and attending movies, which had played a large part in feeding his immorality. He now has an unquenchable desire to study the Bible and pray. And he has remained sexually pure. "It's a miracle!" Rick says. "I have been set free from that lying pimp in my mind."

I believe that every child of God in sexual bondage can experience the freedom Rick has experienced. Jesus broke the power of sin on the cross by defeating the god of this world—Satan, the lying pimp Rick talked about. To appropriate and retain your freedom, you must understand the continuing work of the evil one. He is the lying deceiver at the core of sexual bondage.

Enemy in the Garden

God's plan for the sexual life and health of His human creation has been clear since the beginning.

> The Lord God said, "It is not good for the man to be alone. I will make a helper suitable for him." . . . So the Lord God caused the man to fall into a deep sleep; and while he was sleeping, he took one of the man's ribs and closed up the place with flesh. Then the Lord God made a woman from the rib he had taken out of the man, and he brought her to the man.

> The man said, "This is now bone of my bones and flesh of my flesh; she shall be called 'woman,' for she was taken out of man." For this reason a man will leave his father and mother and be united to his wife, and they shall become one flesh.

> The man and his wife were both naked, and they felt no shame (Genesis 2:18,21-25).

God created Adam in His own image, breathed life into him, and Adam became spiritually and physically alive. Something was missing, however. It wasn't good for Adam to be alone; he needed a suitable helper. None of the animals God had created could adequately fulfill Adam's need. So God created Eve from Adam's rib. The couple was naked and unashamed. There was nothing obscene about their naked bodies. Their sexual relationship was not separated from their intimate relationship with God. There was no sin and nothing to hide, so Adam and Eve had no reason to cover up.

The purpose and responsibility of this first couple was to "be fruitful and increase in number; fill the earth and subdue it" (Genesis 1:28). They were afforded a tremendous amount of freedom as long as they remained in a dependent relationship with God. They had a perfect life and could have lived forever in the presence of God. All their needs were provided for.

But Satan and evil were also present in the universe. The Lord had commanded Adam and Eve not to eat from the tree of the knowledge of good and evil or they would die (Genesis 2:17). But Satan questioned and twisted God's command and tempted the couple through the same three channels of temptation that exist today: "the lust of the flesh and the lust of the eyes and the boastful pride of life" (1 John 2:16 NASB). Deceived by the craftiness of Satan, Adam and Eve defied God, ate of the forbidden fruit, and thus declared their independence from God.

At that moment, Adam and Eve died spiritually, meaning that their intimate relationship with God was severed. In time they also died physically, which is also a consequence of sin (Romans 5:12). But in the intervening years, their perfect life in the garden was ruined by their sin. No longer innocent and without shame, "the eyes of both of them were opened, and they realized they were naked; so they sewed fig leaves together and made coverings for themselves . . . and they hid from the Lord God among the trees of the garden" (Genesis 3:7,8).

The fall affected Adam and Eve's daily life in many ways. First, it darkened their mind. In trying to hide from God, they revealed that they had suddenly lost a true understanding of God. Can you imagine trying to hide from God, who is present everywhere? They were no longer thinking straight. They were darkened in their understanding because they were separated from the life of God (Ephesians 4:18).

Second, the fall affected their emotions. The first emotions expressed by Adam and Eve after the fall—fear and guilt—had never been part of their existence before. When God came looking for the pair, Adam said to Him, "I was afraid [fear] because I was naked [guilt]; so I hid" (3:10).

The fear of being exposed has driven many people from the light that reveals their sin. Without God's unconditional love and acceptance, they are forced to run from the light or discredit its source. Unable to live up to God's eternal standards of morality, they now face the prospect of living in guilt and shame or, like Adam, blaming someone else (Genesis 2:12).

Third, the fall also affected Adam and Eve's will. Before they sinned, they could only make one wrong choice: to eat from the tree of the knowledge of good and evil, which was forbidden to them. Every other choice they could make in the garden was a good choice. However, because Adam and Eve made that one bad choice, they were confronted every day with many good *and* bad choices—just as we are today. We can choose to yield or not yield to a variety of temptations presented to us by the world, the flesh, and the devil. It is the pattern of consistent wrong choices in the area of sexual sin that leads individuals into sexual bondage.

Because of sin, we are totally helpless and hopeless to escape sexual bondage without God. In truth, no person living independently of God can live a moral life or withstand the conviction of His perfect light. "Everyone who does evil hates the light, and will not come into the light for fear that his deeds will be exposed. But whoever lives by the truth comes into the light, so that it may be seen plainly that what he has done has been done through God" (John 3:20,21).

The first step in recovery for anyone in sexual bondage is to come out of the darkness of hiding and face the truth in the light. Many people have told me that they want to get out of sexual bondage because they are tired of living a lie. And bondage to sex is one of the easiest to lie about. For example, the effects of food addiction (either overeating or anorexia and bulimia) show up quickly in the physical appearance of the victim. Drug or alcohol addiction is noticeable within a couple of years. But there are no obvious clues to sexual bondage, unless it surfaces in the form of a sexually transmitted disease. It can remain a private nightmare for a lifetime unless it is brought into the light and dealt with.

A Rebel Takes Control

At the root of the world's dilemma with sin and bondage is Satan. When Adam and Eve sinned, Satan usurped their role as rulers over the earth and became the rebel holder of authority. When Jesus was tempted, Satan offered Him the kingdoms of the world if He would bow down and worship him (Luke 4:6). Jesus didn't dispute

Satan's claim to earthly authority and even referred to him as "the prince of this world" (John 12:31; 14:30; 16:11). Paul called Satan "the prince of the power of the air" (Ephesians 2:2 NASB). As a result of Adam and Eve's fall, "the whole world is under the control of the evil one" (1 John 5:19).

The good news is that God's plan of redemption was underway immediately after Satan wrested authority from Adam and Eve. The Lord cursed the serpent and foretold the downfall of Satan (Genesis 3:14,15), which was accomplished by Christ on the cross. Ultimate authority in heaven and earth now belongs to Him. Satan's days of authority on earth are numbered.

Because we are related to Adam and Eve, all of us were born spiritually dead and were subject to the authority of the prince of this world. But when we received Christ, we were transferred from Satan's kingdom to God's kingdom (Colossians 1:13; Philippians 3:20). Satan is still the ruler of this world, but he is no longer *our* ruler; Jesus Christ is.

However, as long as we live in Satan's world, he will try to deceive us into believing that we belong to him. Even as members of Christ's kingdom we are still vulnerable to Satan's accusations, temptations, and deceptions. If we give in to his tactics, Satan can influence our thinking and behavior. And if we remain under his influence long enough and fail to resist him, Satan can control us in those areas.

That's what happened to Rick, whose story opened this chapter. Before he became a Christian, he formed bad habits in the area of illicit sex. He had traveled the pathways of sexual abuse and sexual promiscuity into sexual bondage. After Rick gave his life to Christ, the pimp in his mind had him convinced that illicit sex was still the answer to his search for love and fulfillment. Only after Rick understood his identity in Christ and exercised his authority in Christ was he able to silence the pimp's lies and break free of his sexual bondage.

The Seeds of Sexual Bondage

So why is this ongoing cosmic battle between God's kingdom and Satan's kingdom, between righteousness and sin, so often waged in the arena of sex and sexual behavior? It dawned on me after years of helping people find their freedom in Christ that a person's sexual practices are a primary way by which seeds are sown in these two kingdoms. For example, most of the people who come to Freedom In Christ Ministries struggling against sin and Satan have some kind of sexual problem. In fact, every person who shared his or her story in my book, *Released from Bondage,* had either been sexually abused, sexually disoriented, or sexually promiscuous.

People who respect and obey God's directives in Scripture regarding sexual purity are sowing seeds in the kingdom of God that will reap a harvest of peace and righteousness. People who ignore God's call to sexual purity are sowing seeds in Satan's kingdom and will reap a harvest of pain and heartache. And the fruit of seeds sown in these two kingdoms greatly impacts our relationships. For example, the seed of pornography was sown in Jon (Chapter 1) and Andy (Chapter 3) by other impure men who were careless with their pornographic magazines, resulting in these boys becoming addicted to pornography. Melissa's grandfather (Chapter 3) sowed seeds of immorality in Satan's kingdom by sexually abusing his granddaughter. The fruit of his sin was Melissa's own sexual bondage.

Satan's primary weapon for ruining relationships is sexual impurity. More Christian marriages and ministries are destroyed because of sexual misconduct than for any other reason. People who are in secret sexual bondage have no joy in marriage or ministry. Conversely, an individual who pursues a life of moral purity is nurturing a crop in the kingdom of God. The result is a positive impact for righteousness on his or her marriage, children, friends, and coworkers.

The strong link between Satan's kingdom of darkness and sexual bondage was illustrated to me during one of my conferences. David was referred to us by the pastoral staff of the host church. He was a successful businessman who appeared to have everything going for him. However, David's wife had just left him because of his pornography addiction. So one of our staff met with him to take him through the Steps to Freedom in Christ (see Appendix A).

As we go through these steps with people, we routinely invite them to renounce any previous involvement in satanic or occult activities, even if they don't remember any. As David renounced making any covenants with Satan, he was shaken to the core when the Lord revealed to him a nightmarish experience from his past. He recalled a frightening encounter with a spiritual being who offered David all the sex and girls he wanted if he would just tell this being he loved Satan. At first David refused, not sure if he was awake or dreaming. Then he gave in and proclaimed his love for Satan. Sowing that seed in Satan's kingdom resulted in the sexual bondage that was ruining David's life and marriage.

After David renounced that experience and completed the Steps to Freedom in Christ, he was free from his bondage to pornography. His life and his marriage are being restored.

Darkness Breeds Impurity

Wherever you find the kingdom of darkness entrenched, you find sexual immorality and perversion flourishing. Several former participants have told me that satanic worship is a degrading and dehumanizing sex orgy. Satanists practice selective breeding to propagate their super race. Inferior offspring are used for sacrifice.

The god of this world has not changed in his debauchery over the centuries. Pagans honored Molech, a detestable Semitic deity, by the fiery sacrifice of children, a practice God strictly prohibited (Leviticus 18:21; 20:1-5). God's people were also warned against worshiping the Babylonian goat idol or satyr (Isaiah 13:21; Revelation 18:2). A satyr is a demon that takes on the form of a shaggy goat. It was especially brutal and lustful in its nature.

There were many other pagan gods in biblical times whose worship involved sexual perversity. Chemosh, the national deity of the Moabites, required the sacrifice of children, and Diana of Ephesus had an explicitly sexual nature. Devotion to any*one* or any*thing* less than the God and Father of our Lord Jesus Christ is idolatry, and idolatry always leads into some perversion of moral purity.

Satan is still in the business of pimping his perversions of God's design for sex and marriage. To find your freedom in Christ, you need not only to understand how the seeds of impurity are sown in the kingdom of darkness, you need to understand God's view of sex. This is the topic of the next chapter.

FIVE

The Phony
and the Genuine

It has been said that the way to learn how to recognize counterfeit money is not to study counterfeit money. You study the real thing—genuine currency—so thoroughly that you will quickly spot a phony bill if you look at it closely. This must also be our approach when contrasting Satan's perversion of sex with God's perfect plan. We should know *something* about the pimp's dark plan and evil methods. But it's the truth that sets us free, not a knowledge of error (John 8:32). It is vital that we understand God's design for sex and marriage in order to walk out of the darkness and sow seeds of righteousness in God's kingdom.

God created us as sexual beings—male and female. Gender is determined at conception, and the entire sexual anatomy is present at birth. Even the molecular structure of a skin sample, when studied under a microscope, will reveal an infant's sexual identity. God is not anti-sex; He created sex! David proclaimed, "You created my inmost being; you knit me together in my mother's womb. I praise you because I am fearfully and wonderfully made; your works are wonderful" (Psalm 139:13,14).

Viewing sex as evil is not an appropriate response to what God created and pronounced good. "Everything God created is good, and nothing is to be rejected if it is received with thanksgiving, because it is consecrated by the word of God and prayer" (1 Timothy 4:4,5). On the other hand, Satan is evil, and sin distorts what God created. Denying our sexuality and fearing open discussion about our sexual development is playing into the devil's hand. A Christian view of sexuality and sexual development, and helpful guidelines for presenting a healthy, biblical view of sex to your children, is found in Appendix B of this book.

A Plan for the Ages

God's ideal plan for marriage was outlined in the Garden of Eden before Adam and Eve sinned: "A man will leave his father and mother and be united to his wife, and they will become one flesh" (Genesis 2:24). Monogamous, heterosexual marriage under God was the divine intention; one man and one woman forming an inseparable union and living in dependence on God.

Adam and Eve were also commanded by God to procreate and fill the earth with their offspring. Had they never sinned, perhaps the world today would be populated with a race of sinless people living in perfect harmony. But Adam and Eve's sin in the garden marred God's beautiful plan. Lest we be too hard on them, however, had any of us been in the garden instead of them, we probably would have done the same thing. Adam and Eve enjoyed ideal conditions and perfect light and still sinned. We could have done no better.

God did not abandon His plan for man, woman, and their sexual relationship despite the fall of Adam and Eve. Rather, He selected the procreative process of human marriage as the vehicle for redeeming fallen humanity. God covenanted with Abraham, "In your seed all the nations of the earth shall be blessed, because you have obeyed My voice" (Genesis 22:18). The "seed" or descendant God was talking about was Christ (Galatians 3:16), who would bless the whole world by providing salvation through His death and resurrection.

There was another facet to God's plan for marriage after the fall. From Adam and Eve to the present, the covenant relationship of marriage between husband and wife has been a God-ordained picture of the covenant relationship between God and His people. The church is called the bride of Christ (Revelation 19:7), and He desires to receive to Himself a bride who is holy and blameless, "without stain or wrinkle or any other blemish" (Ephesians 5:26,27). The purity and faithfulness of a Christian marriage is to be an object lesson of the purity and faithfulness God desires in our relationship with Him.

The Bible prohibits sexual immorality for two interrelated reasons. First, unfaithfulness or sexual sin violates God's plan for the sanctity of human marriage. When you become sexually involved with someone other than your spouse, whether physically or mentally through lust and fantasy, you shatter God's design. You bond with that person, thus blemishing the "one man and one woman" picture and breaking the covenant with your spouse (1 Corinthians 6:16,17). We were created to become one flesh with only one other person. When you commit sexual sin, you become one flesh with every physical or mental partner, resulting in sexual bondage.

That's why Paul calls sexual sin a sin against our own body.

Second, when you commit sexual immorality you deface the picture of God's covenant relationship with His people which your marriage was designed to portray. Think about it: A loving, pure, committed relationship between a husband and wife is God's illustration to the world of the loving, pure, committed relationship He desires with His body, the church. Every act of sexual immorality among His people tarnishes that illustration.

The Plan in the Old Testament

Not many generations passed before the descendants of Abraham found themselves in bondage to Egypt. God raised up Moses to deliver His people and provide for them a law to govern their relationships in the Promised Land, including their sexual relationships. And six of the Ten Commandments listed in Exodus 20 dealt with marital fidelity.

You shall have no other gods before me (v. 3). Illicit sex violates this commandment because it elevates sexual pleasure above our relationship with God. God is a jealous God. He won't tolerate a rival, including the god of our impure appetites.

Honor your father and your mother (v. 12). Sin of any kind, including sexual sin, brings shame and dishonor to our parents.

You shall not commit adultery (v. 14). God ordained sex to be confined to marriage. Adultery—sex outside of marriage—is a sin against your marriage partner and God (Genesis 39:9).

You shall not steal (v. 15). The adulterer robs his spouse of the intimacy of their relationship and steals from his illicit partner sexual pleasure that doesn't belong to him.

You shall not give false testimony (v. 16). Marriage is a covenant made before God and human witnesses. Sexual sin breaks the marriage vow. In effect, the unfaithful partner lies about being faithful to his or her spouse. The adulterer often continues lying to cover up his or her sin.

You shall not covet (v. 17). To covet is to desire something that doesn't belong to you. All sexual sin begins with a desire for someone or some experience that is not rightfully yours.

Though most are delivered in the negative, the commandments of God are not restrictive but protective. God's intention was to prevent a fallen humanity from sowing even more seeds of destruction through sexual immorality and thus enlarging the realm of the kingdom of darkness.

God's law also specified heterosexuality and condemned homosexuality. His people were to maintain a clear distinction between a man and a woman in appearance: "A woman shall not wear men's clothing, nor a man wear women's clothing, for the Lord your God detests anyone who does this" (Deuteronomy 22:5).

Homosexual marriages and sexual relations were also clearly forbidden: "Do not lie with a man as one lies with a woman; that is detestable" (Leviticus 18:22); "If a man lies with a man as one lies with a woman, both of them have done what is detestable. They must be put to death; their blood will be on their own heads" (Leviticus 20:13). God commanded Adam and Eve and their descendants to multiply and fill the earth. The only way they could obey that command was to procreate through the means of sexual intercourse as men and women. Men can't have children by men, and women can't have children by women. The alternative lifestyle of homosexuality is in direct conflict with God's plan of populating the earth, and He detests it.

God also instructed His people regarding the spiritual purity of their marriages: "You shall not intermarry with [pagan nations]; you shall not give your daughters to their sons, nor shall you take their daughters for your sons. For they will turn your sons away from following Me to serve other gods; then the anger of the Lord will be kindled against you, and He will quickly destroy you" (Deuteronomy 7:3,4 NASB).

Ironically, the most glaring example of disobedience to this command is found in the man reputed to be the wisest who ever lived. King Solomon had 700 wives and 300 concubines, including some from the nations with whom God expressly prohibited intermarriage (1 Kings 11:1,2). Solomon was the sad fulfillment of God's prediction: "His wives turned his heart away after other gods; and his heart was not wholly devoted to the Lord his God" (1 Kings 11:4, NASB). We cannot have God-honoring marriages if we seek spouses from outside the circle of God's people.

As I traveled and studied in Israel, I saw a memorial of what happens to the kingdom of God when the king violates God's commandments. Outside the walled city of Jerusalem is a place called "the hill of shame," which is almost completely barren. It was on this hill that King Solomon allowed his foreign wives to build temples to other gods. Israel divided into two nations after the death of Solomon and never returned to the prominence it once enjoyed. The barren hill is a sad reminder of the fruit of disobedience.

The Old Testament also assures us that God designed sex within the confines of marriage for pleasure as well as procreation. The Song of Solomon portrays the joys of physical love in courtship and marriage. Furthermore, the law directed that the first year of marriage should be reserved for marital adjustment and enjoyment: "When a man takes a new wife, he shall not go out with the army, nor be charged with any duty; he shall be free at home one year and shall give happiness to his wife whom he has taken" (Deuteronomy 24:5 nasb).

A Destructive Counterplan

As God's plan of propagation and redemption unfolded in the Old Testament, Satan was there attempting to ruin it.

On one front, he tried to prevent the descendants of Adam and Abraham from producing the Redeemer, Jesus Christ. Satan was behind Pharaoh's order to kill all the male babies when Israel was in bondage to Egypt. But God preserved Moses and raised him up 80 years later to set His people free (Exodus 1,2).

When Christ was born, Herod also tried to annihilate Israel's male babies. But the Lord told Joseph about the plot in a dream, and he took Mary and the infant Jesus to Egypt (Matthew 2:7-23). As we watch the heartless slaughter of millions of unborn children today, we must wonder what great deliverance God has in store for His church and ask, "What is Satan trying to hinder this time?"

Unable to prevent the birth of the Messiah, Satan prompted Judas, one of the Lord's own, to betray Him. That devious plan played right into God's hand. The grave could not hold Jesus, and His resurrection sealed Satan's fate forever.

On another front, Satan went to work to frustrate God's plan for monogamous, heterosexual, God-dependent marriages. Throughout the Old Testament we see the evil one encouraging God's people to ignore His design and sow seeds of destruction through their immorality. Genesis 6:2,4 reports, "The sons of God saw that the daughters of men were beautiful, and they married any of them they chose. . . . The sons of God went to the daughters of men and had children by them."

The "sons of God" were apparently fallen angels. Mark 12:25 states that angels do not procreate after their kind, but on this unique occasion in Genesis 6 it appears that they cohabited with human women to produce human offspring.

How did God respond to this gross perversion of His design? "The Lord saw that the wickedness of man was great on the earth, and that every intent of the thoughts of his heart was only evil continually" (Genesis 6:5). God put an end to that wicked generation by bringing the flood, sparing only Noah and his family. If that evil seedline had continued, who knows what the human race would look like today.

I have counseled many people who have encountered sexual spirits. The Latin terms for male and female sexual spirits are *incubi* and *succubi*. Every period of history records some reference to them. Mythology is replete with stories and images. They have caught the fancy of many artists and sculptors. Incubi and succubi are demon spirits who visit men and women during the night and subject them to sexual depravity, lust, and terrifying nightmares.

Encounters with evil sexual spirits are far more common than most people imagine. We don't hear about them often because such experiences are horribly disgusting and embarrassing. People don't want to admit being confronted by sexual spirits. And these encounters are so bizarre that most people are afraid no one will believe them. Being harassed by a sexual spirit today doesn't produce offspring, but it can result in sexual bondage. Thankfully, in Christ we have the authority to resist all of the devil's schemes.

Satan's assault on God's design of heterosexuality is evident in the account of Sodom and Gomorrah. When angels, appearing as men, visited Lot in Sodom, all the men of the city, young and old, clamored to have them brought outside for a homosexual orgy. God cut off this evil seed-line by destroying the two cities by fire (Genesis 19:1-29). Even today we use the term "sodomy" to describe unnatural acts of sexual intercourse, such as oral and anal sex between males. The AIDS epidemic is a chilling reminder that sowing seeds in Satan's kingdom reaps a tragic harvest.

Israel continued to battle idolatry—and the sexual immorality which always attends it—throughout Old Testament history. When Israel split into two kingdoms— Israel and Judah, both nations went down the tubes spiritually and morally, despite the commandments of the law and the warnings of the prophets. And both nations were judged for their sin. They were conquered by their enemies, and the survivors were deported.

The Old Testament ends on a sad note. Only a remnant of God's people returned from captivity to the land God had given them. For 400 years the stronger neighbor nations pushed them around like bullies. On the eve of Christ's birth the Jews were in political bondage to Rome and in spiritual bondage to their apostate leaders. The glory of God had departed from Israel. Satan had apparently foiled God's plan.

But even though the moral and spiritual fabric of Israel had been shredded, God miraculously preserved her and used her to provide the world's Redeemer. Abraham's seed—Jesus Christ—was about to make His entrance (John 1:14). The blessing of Abraham was soon to be extended to all the nations of the world in Christ.

The Plan in the New Testament

What was God's plan for Christian marriage after the cross in a world still dark with sin? The answer is found in 1 Thessalonians 4:3-5: "This is the will of God, your sanctification; that is, that you abstain from sexual immorality; that each of you know how to possess his own vessel in sanctification and honor, not in lustful passion, like the Gentiles who do not know God" (NASB).

The word "possess" means to acquire or take for yourself. The word "vessel" is rendered "wife" in 1 Peter 3:7. Thus verse 4 can be translated, "That each of you know how to take a wife for himself in sanctification and honor." God's plan is the same in the New Testament as it was in the Old Testament: monogamous, heterosexual marriage under God which is free of sexual immorality. By following God's plan we sow seeds of righteousness in His kingdom for ourselves and future generations. By ignoring God's plan we propagate Satan's agenda in our lives and the lives of others.

My first attempt at discipling a young college man failed miserably. No matter how I tried to help him, he couldn't seem to get his spiritual life together. I was baffled. During that time, he was dating one of the nicest Christian young ladies in the college group. Finally he stopped coming to see me.

Two years later he confessed to me that, while I was trying to disciple him, he was sleeping with several coeds, though not with the nice girl he was dating. He admitted that he had written me off after he heard me talk about sexual purity. He wanted to be a growing Christian, but he wasn't about to give up his secret, sinful activities. No wonder the discipleship process wasn't going anywhere!

Any sexual activity outside God's design is forbidden because it is counterproductive to the process of sanctification. In other words, don't expect to reap the fruit of growth, victory, and fulfillment as a Christian if you are sowing seeds in Satan's kingdom through sexual impurity.

We can apply the instruction in 1 Thessalonians 4 to several specific areas of sexual temptation.

We are to abstain from premarital sex. As already noted, it is quite common in our culture for couples in love to sleep together and even live together before marriage or in lieu of marriage. We hear justifications such as, "Love is what counts; who needs a marriage certificate?" or "How can we know if we're sexually compatible unless we sleep together?" Our world places a high value on physical attraction and sexual compatibility in finding a partner. Christians are far from immune to this influence. During my early years of ministry, 18 of the first 20 Christian couples I counseled prior to marriage admitted to me that they had slept together.

Premarital sexual activity is not God's way for us to seek a life partner. Outward appearance and sexual appeal may be part of the attraction to a potential mate, but neither has the power to hold a couple together. Physical attraction is like perfume. You smell the fragrance when you put it on, but within minutes your sense of smell is saturated and you barely notice the scent

Similarly, unless you go beyond physical attraction to know the real person, the relationship won't last.

Christian dating is not like shopping for a good-looking, comfortable pair of shoes. Shoes get scuffed and worn and dated, and you have to replace them every year or two. Christian dating is the process of finding God's will for a lifetime marriage partner. Commitment to Christ and beauty of character far outweigh physical attraction and sex appeal in importance.

We are to abstain from extramarital sex. Doug and Katy came to see me years ago because they were having marital problems. In an angry moment Doug had told his wife that she didn't satisfy him sexually as a previous girlfriend had. In tears Katy told me how hard she tried to be like that other girl, something which was impossible for her. The couple left my office without resolution.

One day some time later, Doug came home to find Katy sitting on the couch with a pillow on her lap. She asked him if he loved her. Doug said he did. Katy replied, "Then I'm going to make you pay for what you said about me for the rest of your life." She pulled his handgun from under the pillow and shot herself to death.

Marital unfaithfulness is rooted in comparison, which is wrong. You may have been attracted to your mate by his or her appearance, personality, and other qualities. Of all the people you knew, this person seemed made just for you, and you seemed made for him or her. So you committed yourselves to each other "till death do us part."

Once you are married, all comparisons must end. You may meet someone who looks more like a movie star than your spouse, who seems more sensitive and caring, or who may exhibit deeper spiritual fervor. It doesn't matter.

You're with the person God gave you. The best-possible-mate contest is over, and you and your spouse both won! As Christians, our first commitment is to Christ, and this is the most important relationship we have. Your marriage is a picture of that union, and no other relationship must be allowed to deface that picture. The pathway to marital happiness and fulfillment is found in pouring yourself into loving, serving, and fulfilling that person, not in looking for someone you think may bring you greater happiness.

Many people who end up in extramarital affairs say that they were bored with their spouses sexually. They're not bored with their partners; they're bored with sex because they have depersonalized it. When the focus is on the sex act, the partner as a sex object, and personal sexual satisfaction, boredom is likely. But when the focus is on nurturing the total relationship and fulfilling the dreams and expectations of your mate, marital life—including sex—remains an exciting and rewarding experience.

We are not to violate the conscience of our spouse. Several years ago I conducted a one-day conference entitled "For Women Only." The participants were invited to ask me questions on any topic. Embarrassing questions were written out and dropped in a basket. Most of the written questions were about sex, and most of those centered on the question, "Must I submit to anything my husband wants me to do sexually?"

If the real question is, "Should I submit to anything my husband *needs* sexually?" the answer is yes. And the husband should submit to meet his wife's sexual needs also. The definitive passage is 1 Corinthians 7:3-5: "The husband should fulfill his marital duty to his wife, and likewise the wife to her husband. The wife's body does not belong to her alone but also to her husband. In the same way, the husband's body does not belong to him alone but also to his wife. Do not deprive each other except by mutual consent for a time, so that you may devote yourselves to prayer. Then come together again so that Satan will not tempt you because of your lack of self-control."

You are not to withhold sex from your spouse or use it as a weapon against him or her. To do so gives Satan an opportunity to tempt your spouse in areas where he or she lacks self-control.

But should a wife submit to anything her husband *wants* her to do sexually? No. Neither spouse has the right to violate the conscience of the other. If a sexual act is morally wrong for one, it is morally wrong for both. One man protested to me, "But Scripture says that the wedding bed is undefiled." I told him to read the whole verse: "Marriage should be honored by all, and the marriage bed kept pure, *for God will judge the adulterer and all the sexually immoral*" (Hebrews 13:4).

Demanding that your spouse violate his or her conscience to satisfy your lust violates the wedding vow of loving one another and destroys the intimacy of a relationship built on trust. A person can and should meet the legitimate sexual needs of his or her marriage partner. But in no way should your spouse be used to fulfill your lust. It is terribly degrading to demand that your spouse satisfy your lust. The more you feed lustful desires, the more they grow. Only Christ can break that cycle of bondage and give you the freedom to love your wife as Christ loved the church.

We are to abstain from sexual fantasy. There it was again, the thought to pull off the freeway and rent a sexually explicit video. Even though Scott was married with two children still living at home, he still battled the urge to fantasize sexually. He had prayed repeatedly against the impulse, but as he sped closer to the off ramp a conflict raged within him. He knew his actions wouldn't be pleasing to God. He knew he would feel ashamed when it was all over. He knew he would be embarrassed if his wife or children came home unexpectedly and found him acting out his fantasy. But he was propelled to the video store like a heroin addict to a fix.

Scott had found many ways to satisfy his secret craving for sexual excitement and release: pornographic paperback novels and magazines, textbooks on the subject of sexuality, sexual fantasies while in the shower, and steamy videos featuring nudity and sex (he avoided more obvious X-rated films, reasoning that the R-rated ones were easier to explain if he got caught).

Once he took the off ramp Scott was hooked again. He made his selection in the video shop and headed home for an afternoon of self-pleasure. But after watching the movie, he was again flooded with shame and guilt. "How did I get sucked into this pattern again?" he cried. "Lord, what am I going to do?" He had told no one about his ongoing struggle and repeated failure in this area, not his wife, not his pastor, and not the two Christian counselors he had seen in the past for other problems. He felt weak and alone. Even God seemed distant and unavailable.

So Scott did what he always did: He stuffed his feelings and guilt deep inside and went on with the charade of the pure, successful Christian man. Eventually his despair would dissipate and he could relax until the old urges returned and pulled him under again.

The problem of sexual fantasy has surfaced in literally hundreds of Christian men and women I have counseled. These people are not usually physically involved in premarital or extramarital sex. But in their minds they play out an endless variety of sexual adventures with people they know, characters in a raunchy book or magazine or on the video screen, or phantom lovers they dream up on their own. Some sexual fantasy addicts make love to their spouses while secretly imagining that they are with someone else. Others find release in masturbation. Still others seek out illicit affairs.

Sexual fantasy may be regarded by many as harmless self-pleasuring. But Christians are to abstain from it for at least three different reasons.

First, under Jesus' guideline for adultery in Matthew 5:27,28, sexual immorality in the mind carries the same weight as sexual immorality in the flesh: "You have heard that it was said, 'Do not commit adultery.' But I tell you that anyone who looks at a woman lustfully has already committed adultery with her in his heart." You may be able to avoid the personal embarrassment, public scandal, or potential diseases of a physical affair. But in God's eyes an affair in the mind is the same as the real thing. It is a violation of moral purity.

Some people think that looking is what constitutes the act of mental adultery. But the passage teaches that looking only gives evidence that adultery has already been conceived in the heart. We need to heed the instruction of Proverbs 4:23: "Above all else, guard your heart, for it is the wellspring of life."

Second, according to James 1:14,15, sexual immorality in the mind precipitates a sexually immoral act: "Each one is tempted when, by his own evil desire, he is dragged away and enticed. Then, after desire has conceived, it gives birth to sin; and sin, when it is full-grown, gives birth to death." You may think your secret is safe inside you, but "out of the overflow of the heart the mouth speaks" (Matthew 12:34). What is sown and nurtured as a seed in the heart will eventually flower as a deed.

Third, sexual fantasy depersonalizes sex and devalues people. For the person caught up in sexual fantasy, sex is not a facet of mutual joy and sharing in the marital relationship but an avenue for personal pleasure. When sex becomes boring in this person's marriage—which it certainly will with the mentality of all take and no give, he or she must find a more exciting partner, such as a risque picture or story, a steamy video, or an imagined lover.

One man assured me that his sexual fantasizing was not a sin because he visualized girls without heads! I told him, "That's precisely the problem. You have depersonalized sex." This is what pornography does. Sex objects are never regarded as persons created in God's image, much less someone's daughter or son. Treating someone as an object for personal gratification goes against everything the Bible teaches about the dignity and value of human life.

That brings us to the topic of masturbation, a point at which the fantasy world and the physical world meet for many in sexual bondage. Masturbation is seen by some as a harmless, pleasurable means of releasing sexual pressure. Those who practice it, condone it, or recommend it say masturbation is a private, readily available avenue for fully gratifying one's sexual needs without fear of disease or pregnancy.

The Bible is virtually silent on the topic of masturbation, and Christians are widely divided in their opinions about it. Some believe that masturbation is a God-given gift to release pent-up sexual energy when one is unmarried or when one's mate is unavailable. At the other extreme are Christians who condemn masturbation as a sin. Those in favor remind us that it is nowhere condemned in the Bible, that it poses no health risks, and that it may help prevent acts of sexual immorality. Those opposed state that it is sex without a marriage partner and therefore wrong, that it is self-centered, that it often accompanies sexual fantasies, and that it is an uncontrollable habit.

I certainly don't want to add any restrictions that God doesn't intend, nor do I want to contribute to the legalistic condemnation that is already being heaped on people. But why do so many Christians feel guilty after masturbating? Is it because the church or their parents have said it is wrong, and therefore the guilt is only psychological? If so, the condemnation springs from a conscience that has developed improperly. The condemnation may also come from the accuser of the brethren, Satan (Revelation 12:10).

To understand how masturbation may be contributing to your sexual bondage, ask yourself the following questions:

1. Do you employ masturbation as the physical release for your sexual fantasies? If you masturbate as you fantasize about having sex with models in a magazine, characters in a novel or on the screen, or real or imagined persons in your mind, you are only underscoring the mental adultery Jesus condemned.

2. Does masturbation cause you to withhold yourself from your spouse? Paul wrote, "The husband should fulfill his marital duty to his wife, and likewise the wife to her husband. The wife's body does not belong to her alone but also to her husband. In the same way, the husband's body does not belong to him alone but also to his wife" (1 Corinthians 7:3,4). If through masturbation you are

depleting your sexual energy at the expense of your spouse's enjoyment, you are not fulfilling your marital duty.

3. Can you stop masturbating if you want to? If you can't, you may have elevated masturbation, and perhaps your secret life of sexual fantasy, to become a god in your life. God does not tolerate any pretenders to His throne. All idols must be removed.

4. Can you masturbate without visual stimulation (video, magazines, books, etc.) or fantasizing sexually in such a way that you reach orgasm while focusing on someone other than your spouse? I believe such activity constitutes adultery in the mind.

5. Do you sense the Holy Spirit's conviction when you masturbate? Perhaps you are able to masturbate apart from fantasies and from depriving your spouse. Maybe you are not chained to the act by habit; you can stop at will. But if you sense God's urging to stop, that's reason enough.

There is encouraging hope for you if you are trapped in the web of sexual fantasy and uncontrolled masturbation. Scott spent many years struggling against his sexual bondage. But when he recognized that Satan was behind his bondage, he decided to get right with God. Scott walked through the Steps to Freedom in Christ (see Appendix A) and, over a period of months, established a pattern of truth for living his life. The same way of escape is available to you.

As you struggle to gain your freedom in Christ, remember that "there is now no condemnation for those who are in Christ Jesus" (Romans 8:1). Guilt and shame do not produce good mental health; love and acceptance do. God loves you, and He will not give up on you. You may despair in confessing again and again, but His love and forgiveness are unending.

We are to abstain from homosexuality. God's view of homosexuality hasn't changed, even though society seems to be more accepting of this "alternate lifestyle." The New Testament places homosexuality in the same category as other sexual sins we must avoid: "Do not be deceived: Neither the sexually immoral nor idolaters nor adulterers nor male prostitutes nor homosexual offenders nor thieves nor the greedy nor drunkards nor slanderers nor swindlers will inherit the kingdom of God" (1 Corinthians 6:9,10).

Some argue, "But I was born this way. I have always had homosexual tendencies. I can't help it; this is the way God created me." God did not create anyone to be a homosexual. He created us male and female. Homosexuality is a lie. There is no such thing as a homosexual; there is only homosexual behavior. Nor did God create pedophiles, adulterers, or alcoholics. If one can rationalize homosexual behavior, why can't another rationalize adultery, fornication, pedophilia, etc.?

There may be events or influences in your past which have predisposed you to homosexual behavior, just as other seemingly unbidden addictive behaviors, such as alcoholism, can be traced to hereditary, environmental, or spiritual causes beyond the individual's control. But God never commands us to do something we cannot do. He has commanded us to abstain from homosexuality, and He has provided a way of escape. This way of escape from homosexuality and other sexual bondages is covered in Part Two and Appendix A.

For some sick reason, our culture is bent on finding the ultimate sexual experience without regard for whether it is right or wrong. But when they think they've found it, it satisfies only for a season, so the quest must continue. Unfortunately, Christians are negatively influenced by the world's obsession with sex, and such a focus carries painful consequences, as the next chapter describes.

Instead, we should be bent on finding the ultimate personal relationship: "Blessed are those who hunger and thirst for righteousness, for they will be satisfied" (Matthew 5:6). Are you willing to pursue the greatest of all relationships, one that every child of God can have with his heavenly Father? If so, you will be satisfied.

SIX

The Harvest
of Sinful Deeds

Consequences. What goes up must come down. Every action has an equal but opposite reaction. If you jump off a tall building without the benefit of a parachute, hang glider, or bungee cord, you will drop to the sidewalk like a rock. If you plant watermelon seeds in the spring, you'll have watermelons in your garden by summer. Everything we do and every choice we make has built-in consequences. Every seed sown produces a crop.

The same is true of our response to God's plan for sex and marriage. If we sow seeds of sexual purity in our marriages, we will reap the benefits and blessings which come from obedience to God's order. If we sow seeds of sexual immorality, we will reap a dark harvest of negative personal and spiritual consequences. Paul said it this way: "The one who sows to his own flesh shall from the flesh reap corruption, but the one who sows to the Spirit shall from the Spirit reap eternal life" (Galatians 6:8 NASB).

What are the consequences of sowing to the flesh in the area of sexual conduct? What kind of corruption is Paul talking about? First there are the more obvious outward or physical and relational consequences, which we will deal with in this chapter. Second, there are the inward or spiritual consequences, which we will explore in the next chapter. Perhaps one or more of these consequences in your life has arrested your attention and prompted you to turn from sowing to the flesh to finding your freedom and sowing in the Spirit.

The Outward Harvest of Sexual Immorality

Perhaps the most obvious and alarming consequences of ignoring God's design for sex are the physical and relational consequences. Physical pain, the threat of disease and death, and the breakup of a relationship get our attention quickly.

Free sex isn't free, and those who pursue it aren't living in freedom. Sexual promiscuity leads to disgusting forms of bondage, and the potential price tag in terms of health is staggering. Dr. Joe McIlhaney, a gynecologist, states that 30 percent of single, sexually active Americans have herpes. Another 30 percent have venereal wart virus. As many as 30 to 40 percent have chlamydia, which is rampant among teenagers and college students. Cases of gonorrhea and syphilis are increasing at an alarming rate.[1] Medical health experts insist that sexually transmitted diseases (STD's) are by far the most prevalent of communicable diseases. The problem is no longer epidemic but pandemic.

The most frightening aspect of STD's is that they can be passed on without the carrier exhibiting any symptoms. This is especially true for those who test positive for HIV. Victims may go for years without showing signs of illness, unknowingly passing on the disease to their sexual partners who in turn pass it on to other unsuspecting victims. Without medical testing, a person cannot be sure that his or her sexual partner is free of all STD's. Indeed, the partner may not even know he is infected. The rapid spread of STD's in our culture illustrates the chilling truth that a sexual encounter involves more than two people. If you have sex with a promiscuous person, as far as STD's are concerned, you are also having sex with every one of that person's previous sex partners, and you are vulnerable to the diseases carried by all of them.

People who have violated God's design for sex also pay a price in their marriage relationships. Those who have had unholy sex don't seem to enjoy holy sex. I have counseled many women who can't stand to be touched by their husbands due to past illicit sexual experiences. Incredibly, their feelings change almost immediately after finding their freedom in Christ from sexual bondages. One pastor had been snubbed sexually by his wife for ten years because of bondage which had blocked her from sexual intimacy. To their mutual surprise, the couple was able to come together sexually after she found her freedom at one of our conferences.

Promiscuity before marriage seems to lead to lack of sexual fulfillment after marriage. The fun and excitement of sex outside God's will leaves the participant in bondage to illicit encounters and unable to enjoy a normal sexual relationship. If the past sins were consensual, the bondages only increase as the individual attempts to satisfy his or her lust in the marriage bed. If the sins were not consensual, meaning that the person went along with the acts but didn't really want to, he or she is not able to enjoy wholesome marital sex until the past is resolved. These persons lack the freedom to enter into mutual expressions of love and trust.

In cases where persons were victims of severe sexual abuse such as rape or incest, their bodies were used as unwilling instruments of unrighteousness. Tragically, these victims became one flesh with their abusers and have great difficulty relating to their spouses in a normal, healthy way. It's not fair that these people were violated against their will. It's sick, and the sickness pollutes what should be a beautiful and fulfilling marriage relationship. The good news is that people can be set free from the bondage of such violations. They can renounce the unrighteous uses of their body, submit to God, resist the devil, and forgive those who abused them.

In extreme cases of bondage such as satanic ritual abuse, I regularly encounter demonic spirits who claim to be the husbands of their female victims. These women cannot function in a marriage relationship because they have been deceived into believing that they are married to Satan. Rituals that wed a person to Satan are a mockery of Christ's church, because the Bible declares that we are the bride of Christ. When satanic rituals are renounced, the victims are free to grow in their relationships with God and with their spouses.

Defilement of a Family

One of the most heartrending consequences of sexual sin relates to the effect such activities have on the children of the offender. The affair between King David of Israel and Bathsheba, wife of Uriah the Hittite, is a sad case study of the downward steps of personal defilement and its effect on his family. Even though David is called a man after God's own heart (Acts 13:22), he had one dark blot on his life. First Kings 15:5 summarizes his life: "David had done what was right in the eyes of the Lord and had not failed to keep any of the Lord's commands all the days of his life—except in the case of Uriah the Hittite." And because of his moral failure, David's family paid a steep price. Let's consider his steps to defilement and their tragic consequences.

"One evening David got up from his bed and walked around on the roof of the palace. From the roof he saw a woman bathing. The woman was very beautiful, and David sent someone to find out about her" (2 Samuel 11:2,3). There was nothing wrong with the woman, Bathsheba, being beautiful, and there was nothing wrong with David being attracted to her. That's the way God made us. Bathsheba may have been wrong for bathing where others could see her, and David was definitely wrong for continuing to look at her. God provided a way of escape—David could have turned and walked away from the tempting sight. But he didn't take it.

When David sent messengers to get Bathsheba, he was too far down the path of immorality to turn around. They slept together, and she became pregnant. David tried to cover up his sin by calling Uriah, Bathsheba's husband, home from the battlefield to sleep with her. The pregnancy could then be attributed to him. But noble Uriah wouldn't cooperate, so David sent him back to the battle and arranged for him to be killed. Now David the adulterer is also a murderer! Sin has a way of compounding itself. If you think living righteously is hard, try living unrighteously. Cover-up, denial, and guilt make for a very complex life.

After a period of mourning her dead husband, Bathsheba became David's wife. David lived under the guilt and covered his shame for nine months. He apparently suffered physical consequences because of his sin. In Psalm 32:3 he describes his torment: "When I kept silent, my bones wasted away through my groaning all day long. For day and night your hand was heavy upon me; my strength was sapped as in the heat of summer."

The Lord allowed plenty of time for David to come to terms with his sin. The king didn't confess, so God sent the prophet Nathan to confront him. God won't let His children live in darkness for long, because He knows it will eat them alive. One pastor with a pornography addiction traveled to a pastor's conference where colleagues asked for copies of his ministry materials. When the pastor opened the briefcase with a crowd around him, he suddenly realized he had brought the wrong case. His stack of smutty magazines was there for all to see! "There is nothing concealed that will not be disclosed, or hidden that will not be made known" (Matthew 10:26).

Sadly, the public lives of many Christians are radically different from their private lives. As long as they think the facade can continue, they will not deal with their own issues. Ironically, these people are often the ones who are the most critical of others. People who haven't dealt with their own guilt often seek to balance the internal scales by projecting blame on others. But the Lord says in Matthew 7:1-5:

> Do not judge, or you too will be judged. For in the same way you judge others, you will be judged, and with the measure you use, it will be measured to you.
>
> Why do you look at the speck of sawdust in your brother's eye and pay no attention to the plank in your own eye? How can you say to your brother, "Let me take the speck out of your eye," when all the time there is a plank

in your own eye? You hypocrite, first take the plank out of your own eye, and then you will see clearly to remove the speck from your brother's eye.

Forgiveness and Consequences

David finally acknowledged his sins, both of which were capital offenses under the law. Then Nathan said, "The Lord has taken away your sin. You are not going to die. But because by doing this you have made the enemies of the Lord show utter contempt, the son born to you will die" (2 Samuel 12:13,14).

The enemies of the Lord are Satan and his angels. We have little idea of the moral outrage our sexual sins cause in the spiritual realm. Satan, the accuser of the brethren, throws them into God's face day and night (Revelation 12:10). Our private, secret sins are committed openly before the god of this world and his fallen angelic horde! Far worse, our sexual sins are an offense to God, who is grieved by our failure and who must endure the utter contempt of Satan.

The Lord spared David, but his son by Bathsheba had to die. Why? God's law states, "I, the Lord your God, am a jealous God, visiting the iniquity of the fathers on the children, on the third and fourth generations of those who hate Me" (Exodus 20:5 NASB). Is it possible that God had to cut off the rebellious seed that was sown by David so that the male offspring of this adulterous relationship did not receive the birthright? Remember, this is the throne of David upon which the Messiah would eventually reign. Also remember that God is merciful. He took the infant home, and David had the assurance that he would be with the child in eternity (2 Samuel 12:23).

Are succeeding generations guilty for the sins of their parents? Absolutely not! Such was the belief in Israel, but it required a correcting word from the Lord in Ezekiel 18:4: "The soul who sins is the one who will die." Everyone will account for his own sin, but we are all affected by the sins of others. Children are not guilty for their parents' sins, but because their parents sinned, judgment will fall upon them and their household according to the Mosaic covenant. Once a father has set himself against God, this propensity for self-will is likely to be passed to the next generation.

Additional judgment was meted out to David's household as a result of his sin. The prophet Nathan declared, "This is what the Lord says: 'Out of your own household I am going to bring calamity upon you. Before your very eyes I will take your wives and give them to one who is close to you, and he will lie with your wives in broad daylight. You did it in secret, but I will do this thing in broad daylight before Israel'" (2 Samuel 12:11). The Lord's word was fulfilled when Absalom, one of David's sons, "lay with his father's concubines in the sight of all Israel" (2 Samuel 16:22).

Amnon, another son of David, followed his father's example to an even more despicable level of sexual immorality (2 Samuel 13). His lust for his virgin half-sister Tamar, Absalom's sister, provoked him to ply her sympathies with a feigned illness. When Tamar came to his room to take care of him, Amnon tried to seduce her. When she refused, he raped her. Apparently Amnon could have gone through legitimate channels to take Tamar as his wife. But his lust demanded to be satisfied *now*. Additional calamity came upon David as a result of his sin. Four of his sons died prematurely. Bathsheba's son died at birth, Amnon was killed by his brother

Absalom in retaliation for the rape of Tamar, and Absalom and Adonijah were both killed attempting to take the throne from David. All this came upon David because he failed to turn away from the tempting sight of a woman bathing. How important it is to us and our loved ones to take every thought captive to the obedience of Christ (2 Corinthians 10:5).

Is Sin Inherited?

Do we inherit a specific bent toward sin from our parents? And if we do, is this transmission genetic, environmental, or spiritual? I believe the correct answers are *yes* and *all three!* First, there is plenty of evidence to show that we are genetically predisposed to certain strengths and weaknesses. However, genetics cannot be blamed for all bad choices. For example, it has been clearly shown that some people are genetically predisposed to alcoholism. Yet no one is born an alcoholic. People become alcoholics by drinking irresponsibly.

Similarly, some boys possess higher levels of testosterone than other boys, as evidenced by facial hair, body musculature, and obvious masculine traits. Other boys with lower levels of testosterone appear more effeminate. This does not make them homosexuals, but they may be more vulnerable to the possibility, especially if they are severely taunted and teased about their appearance by their peers or parents.

Second, environmental factors also contribute to sinful behavior being passed on from one generation to the next. For example, if you were raised in a home where pornography was readily available and sexual promiscuity was modeled, you would certainly be influenced in this direction. Unless parents deal with their sins, they unwittingly set up the next generation to repeat their moral failures. "A student is not above his teacher, but everyone who is fully trained will be like his teacher" (Luke 6:40).

Third, there seems to be an inherited spiritual bent toward sin as well. For instance, Abraham lied about his wife, calling her his sister. Later his son Isaac did exactly the same thing. Then Isaac's son Jacob lied in order to steal his brother's birthright. After Abraham's falsehood, his offspring appear to be spiritually predisposed to falsehood.

We are not just up against the world and the flesh in our struggle to find our freedom in Christ. Scripture tells of a third unwanted contributor to our makeup: Satan. Jeremiah 32:17,18 declares, "Ah, Lord God! Behold, Thou hast made the heavens and the earth by Thy great power and by Thine outstretched arm! Nothing is too difficult for Thee, who showest lovingkindness to thousands, but repayest the iniquity of the fathers into the bosom of their children after them, O great and mighty God."

Notice that the sins of the fathers are repaid into the bosom of their children. This is not an environmental or genetic factor; this is an intergenerational factor based on the disobedience of ancestors. This unholy inheritance cannot be dealt with passively. We must consciously take our place in Christ and renounce the sins of our ancestors. We are not guilty of our parents' sins, but because they sinned, their sins may be passed on to us. That is why we are told in Leviticus 26:40 to confess our own sin and the sin of our forefathers "in their unfaithfulness which they have committed against Me, and also in their acting with hostility against Me." The opposite is to cover up and defend the sins of our parents, grandparents, etc. and continue in the cycle of bondage.

The possibility of overcoming generational sins is evidenced in the life of Joseph, one of Jacob's sons. Joseph was given every opportunity to lie to protect himself from his jealous brothers. In fact, the more he told the truth, the more trouble he endured. If he was predisposed to lying, he chose not to comply. Eventually he was totally vindicated for his honesty.

I frequently minister to people who repeat the sins of their parents and grandparents. Are they forced to do these things? No! But they will repeat them if they continue to hold iniquity in their hearts, which can be visited to the third and fourth generations.

No matter what our ancestors have done, if we repent and believe in Christ, God rescues us from the dominion of darkness and brings us into the kingdom of His dear Son (Colossians 1:13). We are under a new covenant which promises, "Their sins and lawless acts I will remember no more" (Hebrews 10:17).

Repentance Breaks the Chain

Repentance is God's answer to iniquity, whether ours or our ancestors'. To repent means to have a change of mind about sin, from active or passive participation to renunciation. Repentance is far more than mental acknowledgment, however. It means to turn from our wicked ways and trust in God. It means to no longer hold iniquity in our hearts. The early church began their public profession of faith by declaring, "I renounce you, Satan, and all your works and ways." This would be a good statement to add to our daily confession of faith in Christ. The idea is to reclaim any ground we or our forefathers have given to

Satan. Then we commit all we have and all we are to God. In this way we are being faithful stewards of everything God has entrusted to us (1 Corinthians 4:1,2).

Such a commitment should include our possessions, our ministries, our families, and the activity of our physical bodies, including sexual activity. As we renounce any previous use of these for the service of sin and then dedicate them to the Lord, we are saying that the god of this world no longer has any right over them. They now belong to God, and Satan can't have them or use them.

It is important to understand that God forgives us when we repent, but He doesn't necessarily take away the consequences of our sin. If He did, it wouldn't take us long to figure out that we can sin all we want and then turn to God for cleansing without any repercussions.

It is also important to realize that when a parent repents there is no guarantee that his or her children will. Even if they were influenced genetically, environmentally, or spiritually in the direction of your sin, your children are responsible for their own choices. They may choose to repeat or not to repeat your failures. If they do follow you into sin, they may choose or not choose to follow your example of repentance.

Bad health is contagious, but unfortunately good health isn't. Paul wrote, "Do not be misled: 'Bad company corrupts good character'" (1 Corinthians 15:33). Your children may have "caught" your bad habits from you, but they won't necessarily catch repentance from you. However, your repentant, healthy, God-fearing lifestyle may influence them to make their own choice to renounce sin and trust Christ.

David's sexual sin and murderous cover-up was tragic, and the consequences of sin in his own life and in the lives of his children were painful and long-lasting. But his story has a happy ending. David responded to his sin correctly and went on to shepherd Israel with integrity of heart and lead them with skillful hands (Psalm 78:72). And his seed-line provided the human component to the Satan-crushing Redeemer promised in Genesis 3:15.

David's confession of sin in Psalm 51 is a model prayer for those who violate God's plan for sex:

> Have mercy on me, O God, according to your unfailing love; according to your great compassion blot out my transgressions. Wash away all my iniquity and cleanse me from my sin. For I know my transgressions, and my sin is always before me. Against you, you only, have I sinned and done what is evil in your sight, so that you are proved right when you speak and justified when you judge.... Create in me a pure heart, O God, and renew a steadfast spirit within me. Do not cast me from your presence or take your Holy Spirit from me. Restore to me the joy of your salvation and grant me a willing spirit, to sustain me (verses 1-4, 10-12).

But what if we sin and don't confess? What if we get caught up in pornography, lust, sexual fantasy, or illicit affairs and keep it a secret instead of exposing it to the light? What kind of consequences can we expect?

In addition to exacerbating the physical and relational consequences described in this chapter, continued sexual sin leads us down a dark path to the dead end of sexual bondage. The next chapter describes this process and prepares us for finding the way of escape in Part Two.

SEVEN

The Dark Dead End of Bondage

A second look at the story of Amnon's rape of his half sister Tamar, briefly described in the last chapter, introduces the most sobering of all consequences of sexual sin: bondage.

Before the act, "Amnon son of David fell in love with Tamar. . . . Amnon became frustrated to the point of illness on account of his sister Tamar, for she was a virgin, and it seemed impossible for him to do anything to her" (2 Samuel 13:1,2). What Amnon called love was really lust, as evidenced by his selfish behavior.

Solomon warned in Proverbs 6:25,26, "Do not lust in your heart after her beauty or let her captivate you with her eyes, for the prostitute reduces you to a loaf of bread, and the adulteress preys upon your very life." Tamar was not a prostitute, but the sexual fantasy in Amnon's mind had been replayed so many times that he was physically sick. He had looked lustfully once too often. The way of escape was gone. He had probably slept with her in his mind many times. This kind of lust screams for expression.

So Amnon and his friend Jonadab concocted a plan to get Tamar into Amnon's bed.

Once a plan to fulfill the demands of lust is set in motion, it can seldom be stopped. Amnon had lost control, and where there is no self-control all reason is gone. Amnon's sick desire had reduced him to a loaf of bread—powerless to stop the runaway train of his desires. Tamar's description was correct: Amnon was "like one of the wicked fools in Israel" (2 Samuel 13:13).

Ironically, right after the act, "Amnon hated her with intense hatred. In fact, he hated her more than he had loved her. Amnon said to her, 'Get up and get out!'" (2 Samuel 13:15). It's clear that Amnon wasn't in love; he was trapped in a cycle of sexual addiction. All people in bondage hate the things that control them. The alcoholic craves a drink, then when he's had his fill he smashes the bottle against the wall in remorse, only to go buy another when the craving returns. The pornography addict burns his magazines, tosses his X-rated videos into the garbage, or tells his secret playmate he never wants to see her again. But when his lust rekindles—as it always does, he's back to his old haunts looking for a sexual fix. The most debilitating consequence of repeatedly yielding to sexual temptation and sin is the cycle of sexual addiction it leads to.

The Addiction Cycle

The addiction cycle is basically the same for every form of bondage, including sexual bondage. The cycle involves an individual's baseline experience of sexual behavior. Activities above the baseline are acceptable or

The Addiction Cycle

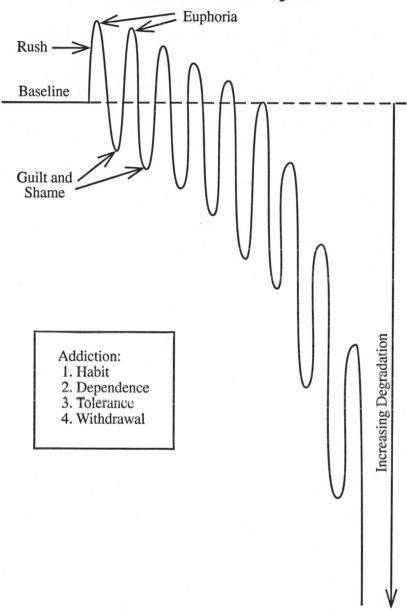

right in the eyes of the individual. Activities below the line are considered questionable or wrong. For the Christian, the area above the baseline represents God's plan for sexual purity, and the area below the line represents sexual impurity.

Each loop of the cycle represents a sexual thought or action with several stages. The emotional or physical rush prompted by the experience surges to a euphoric high, followed by a decline. For example, Joe, a teenaged boy, notices a new girl in class, Mary, a real beauty. Joe feels a rush of emotion just looking at Mary. When Mary returns his glance with a smile, Joe's face flushes warm and his heart races with excitement. He's never felt so high. When the bell rings and Mary walks out of class, Joe's feelings decline. It's over for now, but he liked what he felt. He can't wait to see Mary again and repeat the sensational high.

All week long Joe watches Mary in class with the same wonderful, exciting results. Now, Joe is a nice Christian boy, and he has his standards of sexual purity. He has Mary's best interests at heart. But Joe craves more of that glorious high. So he invites Mary on a date.

Riding in the car with Mary brings a tremendous rush. When she innocently reaches over and touches his leg, Joe almost flies out the top! They hold hands and end the date with a light hug. Joe is in love. So far, so good. He has not compromised his standards. But he begins to imagine what it might feel like if they went a little farther.

Before long a hug and then a kiss from Mary don't give Joe the same rush they first did. To have the same euphoric experience, Joe has to become a little more adventurous. However, going farther means he has to compromise his moral convictions a little. Joe is more free with his hands during their passionate good night kisses. When he's alone he begins to fantasize about touching and kissing other parts of Mary's body.

At first stepping over the line was worth it to Joe. The immediate gratification was wonderful. But as the euphoria declines, Joe's conscience kicks in with twinges of guilt and shame. So he quickly overcomes these negative feelings with more sexual thoughts and experiments. Every new compromise brings greater conviction, which introduces greater compromise. At this point, Joe—and perhaps Mary as well—is well on his way to being locked into a downward-spiraling addictive cycle.

The same cycle operates for other forms of sexual addiction: pornography, sexual fantasy, homosexuality. Like a drug, seemingly harmless injections of euphoria wear off and call for greater doses. As lust grows, more experience is required to quench it. But it can't be satisfied. The more a fleshly desire is fed, the larger it grows. Normal sexual experiences don't seem to bring the euphoria that a simple touch once did. So other experiences must be tried to get that same high. Self-centered thinking begins to dominate. The conviction to not violate another's conscience or moral boundaries is replaced by "How far can I get her to go?"

As the decline continues, a sexual habit brings an increasing sense of dependence on the experience. The pleasurable act becomes a means of releasing stress and tension. There is an increased tolerance for sin as the mind is repeatedly filled with pornographic images and actual experiences. Most people in sexual bondage begin to withdraw from people and from God as the degradation continues. The unchecked cycle of sexual addiction eventually opens the door to sexually transmitted diseases and even death. Addicts with a strong conscience against violating others will turn to self-gratification. Pornography and uncontrolled masturbation become a vicious cycle of habitual experience.

Fear and danger replace love and trust in the search for greater sexual highs. A married man shared that he filled his craving for "exciting" sex by carrying on an adulterous affair in a motel. He and his girlfriend liked to perform sex with the curtains open or late at night in the motel swimming pool. For this man, sex with his Christian wife had become unexciting because his lust was reinforced by fear and danger.

A Spiritual Battle

The shameful decline of sexual addiction is depicted in Romans 1:24-28:

> Therefore God gave them over in the sinful desires of their hearts to sexual impurity for the degrading of their bodies with one another. They exchanged the truth of God for a lie, and worshiped and served the created things rather than the Creator—who is forever praised. Amen.

> Because of this, God gave them over to shameful lusts. Even their women exchanged natural relations for unnatural ones. In the same way the men also abandoned natural relations with women and were inflamed with lust for one another. Men committed indecent acts with other men, and received in themselves the due penalty for their perversion.

> Furthermore, since they did not think it worthwhile to retain the knowledge of God, he gave them over to a depraved mind, to do what ought not to be done.

If you find yourself in this downward spiral, realize that your degradation began when you exchanged the truth of God for a lie and began worshiping created things rather than the Creator. In a moment of temptation, you chose to follow lustful desires instead of God's plan for sexual purity. With every repeated negative choice, the lie became more deeply entrenched. Satan, the "father of lies" (John 8:44), couldn't be more pleased.

There are many ways by which we are tempted to exchange the natural for the unnatural in the area of sexual behavior. One is the fascination with oral and anal sex. Before the so-called sexual revolution of the '60s, those acts were considered to be sodomy in almost every state in the union. Even today the media uses the term "sodomy" for forced oral sex. Our young people are experimenting with oral sex because they consider it "safe," that is, they can't get pregnant. But it's not safe in a time when sexually transmitted diseases are rampant.

Can oral and anal sex be considered natural uses of our bodies? Is that how God designed those body parts to be used? From the standpoint of hygiene only, is it natural to put the mouth so close to the orifices for bodily elimination? Scripture is silent on this specific issue. We are left to determine what is natural and unnatural based on the Holy Spirit's guidance. If a Christian couple mutually agrees that oral sex is a holy use of your body, so be it.

Ignorance of the truth is no excuse. God has designed us with a built-in tracking system that directs us toward appropriate moral conduct (Romans 1:18-20). If we stubbornly ignore this system, God permits the kingdom of darkness to further blind us to the truth. This results in the overthrow of God the Creator as King in favor of almighty self, the creature.

Operating on the basis of a lie, the individual denies that his unrighteous behavior is wrong. Every conscious choice against the truth numbs the soul's awareness of it. Behaviors that were once seen as unnatural and indecent are passionately accepted as normal. The conscience becomes seared and any knowledge of God is gradually blotted out.

God brings judgment upon those who will not honor Him. He gives them over to their degrading passions. When the church at Corinth condoned an incident of sexual perversion, Paul instructed them, "Hand this man over to Satan, so that the sinful nature may be destroyed and his spirit saved on the day of the Lord" (1 Corinthians 5:5).

Throughout this degenerative process, God graciously provides a way of escape through Christ. No matter where a person may be in his or her flight from the truth into darkness, there is a way out. The serial rapist and murderer on death row is just as welcome to God's forgiveness and deliverance as the child who lies about stealing a cookie. In God's economy, sin is not measured in quality or quantity. Jesus paid the price for all of it. Freedom from sexual bondage is available to everyone.

Notice the progression that Paul gives in Romans 1: from shameful lusts to homosexuality to a depraved mind. As a nation, America is probably between stages two and three. Homosexuality is accepted as an alternative lifestyle and protected by our courts. Our minds are becoming increasingly depraved. The frightening thing is that a depraved mind is devoid of logic. It can no longer reason morally. We are well on our way to sliding completely off our moral foundation as a nation.

Is there hope for those who haven't gone too far? Can we repent of our sinful ways and return to God? Of course we can, and we can have victory over sin if we understand and appropriate our position in Christ, as Part Two explains.

Strongholds in the Mind

Another way to view the dark, dead-end consequence of sexual bondage is to understand how strongholds are erected in the mind. Remember: A stronghold is an established, habitual pattern of thinking and behaving against which the individual is virtually powerless to choose or act. The formation of these strongholds occurs in two ways, often beginning early in life.

The first avenue is through the *prevailing experiences* in our lives, such as families, friends, churches, neighborhoods, jobs, etc. As children, our attitudes and actions were partially shaped by each of these influences. For example, friends who shared their pornographic magazines with you may have encouraged you into a fascination with or addiction to pornography. Or if a relative sexually abused you as a child, those experiences have influenced your thinking and behavior. Even into adulthood our day-to-day environment helps shape how we live.

Environment isn't the only prevailing experience which determines how we develop. Two children can be raised in the same home by the same parents, eat the same food, play with the same friends, and attend the same church and still respond differently to life. We are individually created expressions of God's workmanship (Psalm 139:13,14; Ephesians 2:10). Despite similarities in genes and upbringing, our particular differences make our responses to the world around us unique.

The second great contributor to the development of strongholds in our minds is *traumatic experiences.* Whereas prevailing experiences are assimilated by the mind over time, one traumatic experience can be instantly burned into our memory because of its intensity. For example, one bad encounter with a nest of hornets may leave a child with a deep fear of all flying, stinging insects as an adult. Perhaps you were raped as a child or teenager. Or maybe your parents were divorced, or one of them died suddenly. All of these traumatic experiences are stored in our memory bank and influence our thinking.

As we struggle to reprogram our minds against the negative input of past experiences, we are also confronted daily with an ungodly world system. Paul warned us, "Do not conform any longer to the pattern of this world" (Romans 12:2). As Christians we are not immune to worldly values; we can allow them to affect our thinking and behavior. But Paul insisted, "Don't let them influence you!" He also instructed, "See to it that no one takes you captive through hollow and deceptive philosophy, which depends on human tradition and the basic principles of this world rather than on Christ" (Colossians 2:8).

Since we live in this world, we will continuously face the temptation to conform to it. It is not a sin to be tempted. If it were, Christ was the worst sinner who ever lived, because He was "tempted in every way, just as we are— yet was without sin" (Hebrews 4:15). We sin when we consciously choose to give in to temptation.

All temptation is an attempt by Satan to get us to live our lives independently of God, to walk according to the flesh rather than according to the Spirit (see Galatians 5:16-23). Satan knows exactly which buttons to push when tempting us. He knows your weaknesses and your family history. He's aware of the prevailing experiences and traumatic experiences which have made you vulnerable to certain temptations. And based on your past behavior, he knows how to tantalize you to entertain impure thoughts and deeds.

Each temptation begins with a seed thought planted in our minds by the world, the flesh, or the devil himself. Since we live in Satan's world, we must learn how to stand against the temptations he throws at us. Since sex is used in the media to entertain and to sell everything from beer to deodorant to toothpaste to cars, we are constantly bombarded with seed thoughts perverting God's plan for sex. Many people can be tempted to sexual sin without much prompting from the external world, because they have programmed so much junk into their minds through TV, movies, books, and magazines. They can fantasize for years without leaving their homes.

That's why sexual strongholds are so difficult to overcome. Once they are formulated in the mind, the mental pictures are there for instant recall. An alcoholic can't get drunk by fantasizing about a bottle. A drug addict can't get high by imagining himself snorting cocaine. A habitual overeater isn't soothed thinking about a giant chocolate cake. But some victims of sexual bondage can get a rush, a high, and even a self-induced orgasm without any external props. Of course, pornography and illicit sexual activities serve to reinforce and strengthen sexual strongholds.

Strongholds in the Mind

If we continue to act on wrong choices in response to temptation, a habit can be formed in about six weeks. If the habit persists, a stronghold will be developed in the mind. My friend Ed Silvoso says, "A stronghold is a mindset impregnated with hopelessness that causes one to accept as unchangeable something known to be contrary to the will of God."

Strongholds are mental habit patterns that have been burned into our minds over time or by the intensity of traumatic experiences. They are evident in temperament and behavior that is less than Christlike, as illustrated by three common strongholds: inferiority, alcoholism, and homosexuality.

Inferiority is a major stronghold that most Christians struggle with. We don't develop an inferiority complex overnight; it is burned into our minds over time. If you are plagued by feelings of inferiority, chances are you were raised under a harsh performance code. No matter how hard you tried, you couldn't please your parents, your teachers, your pastor, or God. Your efforts were never quite good enough.

As a redeemed child of God, you understand that you are inferior to no other person. But the deeply ingrained feelings of the past won't let you act on the truth. You feel trapped on a dead-end street. So you are constantly searching for the acceptance that eluded you as a child. That's a stronghold. It must be demolished for you to walk in the freedom of who you are in Christ.

Look at the strongholds that come from living in an alcoholic home. Three boys are raised by a father who becomes an alcoholic after years of drinking. The man comes home drunk and abusive every night. His oldest boy is strong enough to stand up to Dad. There is no way he is going to take anything from this drunk. The middle boy doesn't think he can stand up to Dad, so he accommodates the man, tries to comfort him. The youngest boy is terrorized. When Dad comes home he heads for the closet or hides under the bed.

Twenty years later the father is gone and these three boys are now adults. When they are confronted with a hostile situation, how do you think they respond? Of course, the older one fights, the middle one accommodates, and the younger one runs and hides. Those are strongholds in the mind—mental habit patterns of thought that have developed over time.

Similarly, sexual strongholds are the dark dead end of sexual temptation, sexual sin, and impure habit patterns. You may *know* about God's plan of sexual purity and even *agree* with it. But, try as you might, you can't *conform* to it. You are likely trapped in one of the following sexual strongholds.

Homosexuality is a major stronghold, probably one of the most resistant to normal treatment. Those who are caught in the web of this stronghold weren't born that way. Homosexuality itself is a lie. There is no such thing as a homosexual. God created us male and female. There is only homosexual behavior, which the Lord condemns. Condemning those who struggle with this behavior, however, will prove counterproductive. They don't need any more condemnation. They suffer from an incredible identity crisis already. Overbearing authoritarianism is what drove many to this lifestyle in the first place.

Most of those who struggle with homosexual tendencies or behaviors have had poor developmental upbringing. Sexual abuse, dysfunctional families (often where the roles of mother and father are reversed), exposure to homosexual literature before they had an opportunity to fully develop their own sexual identity, playground teasing, and poor relationships with the opposite sex all contribute to their mental and emotional development. Mixed messages lead to mixed emotions.

Charles, a 52-year-old pastor, admitted to me that he had struggled with homosexual tendencies for as long as he could remember. More than once he had given in to those urges. He begged God to forgive him and take the feelings away. He had attended healing services and self-help groups for those with sexual bondages. Nothing worked. To his credit, Charles never once got mad at God. He was married and somehow had kept his struggle a secret from his family. Most people in sexual bondage struggle privately. It is an extremely lonely battle.

I asked Charles what his earliest childhood memory was. He went right back to the age of two. His birth father left before he was born, and his Christian mother raised him. She had a boyfriend who occasionally came over and spent the night. On those nights two-year-old Charles had to share a bed with this man. Charles' earliest childhood memory was of this man, whom he admired so much, turning his back to him and going to sleep. The little boy was desperately looking for affirmation from a male figure, wanting so much to be loved, accepted, and appreciated. As an adult he found that affection in homosexual men.

As I walked him through the Steps to Freedom in Christ, Charles broke down and cried. He forgave his birth father for abandoning him and forgave the man who slept in his bed for rejecting him. Then he renounced every sexual use of his body as an instrument of unrighteousness and gave himself and his body to the Lord. I also encouraged him to renounce the lie that he was a homosexual and declare the truth that God had created him to be a man. As he finished the Steps, the bondage to homosexuality was broken.

I didn't cast a demon of homosexuality out of him. I don't believe there is a demon of homosexuality or a demon of lust. That kind of simplistic thinking has hurt the credibility of the church. I have seen Christianity mocked on prime-time television by a parade of homosexuals and lesbians who have left the church because well-meaning Christians have tried to cast a demon of homosexuality out of them.

Don't get me wrong: There is no question that Satan is behind their problem, and his demons will tempt, accuse, deceive, and take advantage of any ground that is given to them. Focusing on the demonic only deals with part of the problem. It doesn't take into consideration all the other factors, and I personally don't think that method of dealing with the demonic is best.

We have identified God's beautiful design for sex and marriage. We have seen how Satan attempts to pervert God's design and direct our attention away from the Creator to self and its desires. We have considered the contributing factors to sexual bondage and listed the steps which lead to this dark dead end. Hopefully you have gained insight into the reasons for your struggles in the area of sexual purity.

But that's only half the story. The best is yet to come. There is a way out of the dark, suffocating prison of sexual bondage. That way out is Jesus Christ. His provision for our freedom is the theme of Part Two.

PART TWO

The Way
of Escape

EIGHT

Beliefs that Open Prison Doors

So if God's Word so clearly and strongly commands people not to live in sexual bondage, why don't we just obey God and stop doing what He forbids? Because telling people that they are doing wrong does not give them the power to stop doing it. Paul declared, "If a law had been given that could impart life, then righteousness would certainly have come by the law. But the Scripture declares that the whole world is a prisoner of sin" (Galatians 3:21,22). The law is powerless to eliminate the problem and give life. Something more is needed.

Even more discouraging is Paul's statement, "The sinful passions aroused by the law were at work in our bodies" (Romans 7:5). The law not only can't help us do right, it actually has the capacity to provoke what it is trying to prohibit. Forbidden fruit always appears more desirable. If you don't believe it, tell your child he can go *here* but he can't go *there*. Where does he immediately want to go? *There!* Laying down the law does not remove sinful passions. The core problem is the basic nature of people, not their behavior.

The Pharisees were the most law-abiding people of Jesus' day, but they were far from righteous. Jesus told His disciples, "Unless your righteousness surpasses that of the Pharisees and the teachers of the law, you will certainly not enter the kingdom of heaven" (Matthew 5:20). Jesus' Sermon on the Mount confronts the issue of genuine righteousness which is determined by the condition of the heart. For example, He taught, "You have heard that it was said, 'Do not commit adultery.' But I tell you that anyone who looks at a woman lustfully has already committed adultery with her in his heart" (Matthew 5:27,28). A person doesn't commit adultery when he or she looks; the looking just gives evidence that adultery was already committed in the heart.

Jesus goes on to say, "If your right eye causes you to sin, gouge it out. . . . If your right hand causes you to sin, cut it off" (verses 29,30). Do our eyes and hands cause us to sin? Not really. Getting rid of them may be necessary if our only option is to live under the law. But if we keep cutting off body parts to stop sinning, we will end up as dismembered torsos rolling down the street—and we will still have to deal with lust in our hearts. No, taking cold showers to put out the fires of lust and walking blindfolded on a sunbathers' beach may bring temporary relief, but it does not deal with the condition of the heart.

Trying to live a righteous life externally when we are not righteous internally will only result in us becoming "whitewashed tombs, which look beautiful on the outside but on the inside are full of dead men's bones and everything unclean" (Matthew 23:27). The focus must be on what is inside: "For from within, out of men's hearts, come evil thoughts, sexual immorality, theft, murder, adultery, greed, malice, deceit, lewdness, envy, slander, arrogance, and folly. All these evils come from inside and make a man 'unclean' " (Mark 7:20-23).

The Secret of Victory

If trying harder to break the bonds of lustful thoughts and behavior and to live in sexual purity doesn't work, what will? Two verses in the Bible succinctly state what must happen in order for us to live righteously in Christ: "The reason the Son of God appeared was to destroy the devil's work. No one who is born of God will continue to sin, because God's seed remains in him" (1 John 3:8,9). If you are going to be set free from sexual bondage and walk in that freedom, your basic nature must be changed, and you must have a means for overcoming the evil one.

For those of us who are Christians, these conditions have already been met. God has made us partakers of His divine nature (2 Peter 1:4) and provided the means by which we can live in victory over sin and Satan.

Before we knelt at the cross, the following words described us: "You were dead in your trespasses and sins, in which you formerly walked according to the course of this world, according to the prince of the power of the air, of the spirit that is now working in the sons of disobedience. Among them we too all formerly lived in the lusts of our flesh, indulging the desires of the flesh and of the mind, and were by nature children of wrath" (Ephesians 2:1-3 NASB). Before Christ, we were dead in our sins and subject to the control of Satan.

But a change took place at salvation. Paul wrote, "You were once darkness, but now you are light in the Lord" (Ephesians 5:8). Our old nature in Adam was darkness; our new nature in Christ is light. We have been transformed at the core of our being. We are no longer "in the flesh"; we are "in Christ." Paul wrote, "Those who are in the flesh cannot please God. However you are not in the flesh but in the Spirit, if indeed the Spirit of God dwells in you" (Romans 8:8,9 NASB).

Furthermore, before we became Christians we were under the dominion of the god of this world, Satan. But at salvation God "rescued us from the dominion of darkness and brought us into the kingdom of the Son he loves, in whom we have redemption, the forgiveness of sins" (Colossians 1:13,14). We no longer have to obey the evil prompting of the world, the flesh, and the devil. We "have been given fullness in Christ, who is the head over every power and authority" (Colossians 2:10). We are free to obey God and walk in righteousness and purity.

There is no way we can fix the failure and sin of the past, but by the grace of God we can be free from it. God's Word promises, "If anyone is in Christ, he is a new creation; the old has gone, the new has come!" (2 Corinthians 5:17). Furthermore, we are seated with Christ in the heavenlies, far above Satan's authority (Ephesians 2:4-6; Colossians 2:10,11), paving the way for us to live in victory and freedom over sin and bondage. But we also have a responsibility. We must *believe* the truth of who we are in Christ and change how we *walk* as children of God to conform to what is true.

Paul writes in Ephesians 1:18,19, "I pray also that the eyes of your heart may be enlightened in order that you may know the hope to which he has called you, the riches of his glorious inheritance in the saints, and his incomparably great power for us who believe." We already share in Christ's rich inheritance, and we already have the power to live victoriously in Christ. God has provided these glorious benefits for us. The problem for most Christians struggling in bondage is that they just don't see it.

As you work through Part Two of this book, my prayer is that the eyes of your heart will be opened to see the inheritance and power God has provided for you in Christ. In this chapter you will discover what you must *believe* to find the way of escape from sexual bondage. In Chapter 9 you learn how to *walk* in accordance with that liberating belief.

Alive in Christ and Dead to Sin

Before examining our position in Christ from the book of Romans, let me clarify some basic principles of Bible interpretation. When you come to a command in the Bible, the only proper response is to obey it. But when Scripture is expressing something that is true, the only proper response is to believe it. It's a simple concept, but people often get it twisted by trying to do something God only expects them to believe and accept as truth before living accordingly by faith.

Nowhere is this more likely to occur than in Romans 6:1-11, which is explored in this chapter. Many Christians read this section and ask, "How do I do that?" Romans 6:1-11 is not something you can do; it's only something you can believe. But believing it will totally affect your walk by faith. It is the critical first step to finding the way of escape from sexual bondage.

Another principle of Bible interpretation to understand is that the New Testament Greek language is very precise, especially when it comes to verb tenses. You can know when a verb is past, present, or future tense, and whether the verb is describing continuous action or an action which occurred at a point in time. However, you don't have to know the Greek language to appreciate what the Word of God is saying. The English translations bring this out fairly well, although sometimes the verb tenses are not quite as obvious.

Applying these principles to Romans 6:1-11, we discover several specific truths we are called to believe about ourselves, sin, and God. These beliefs form the foundation for the believer's hope in overcoming sin and bondage, including sexual bondage.

You Are Dead to Sin

"What shall we say, then? Shall we go on sinning so that grace may increase? By no means! We died to sin; how can we live in it any longer?" (Romans 6:1,2). The defeated Christian asks, "How do I do that? How do I die to sin, including the sexual sins which have me bound?" The answer is, "You can't do it!" Why not? Because you have already died to sin at salvation. "We died to sin" is past tense; it has already been done. This is something you must believe, not something you must do.

"I can't be dead to sin," you may respond, "because I don't *feel* dead to sin." You will have to set your feelings aside for a few verses, because it's what you believe that sets you free, not what you feel. God's Word is true whether you choose to believe it or not. Believing the Word of God doesn't make it true; His Word is true, therefore you must believe it even if your emotions don't cooperate.

A pastor stopped by my office one day and said, "I have been struggling for 22 years in my Christian experience. It's been one trial after another, and I think I know what my problem is. I was doing my devotions the other day when I came across Colossians 3:3, 'For you died, and your life is now hidden with Christ in God.' That's the key to victory, isn't it?" I assured him that I agreed. Then he asked, "How do I do that?"

I was surprised by his question, so I asked him to look at the passage again and read it just a little slower. So he read it again: "For you died, and your life is hidden with Christ in God." Again he asked in desperation, "I know I need to die with Christ, but how do I do it?" This dear man has been desperately trying for 22 years to do something that has already been done, to become someone he already is. He's not alone. Many Bible-believing Christians are bogged down in their maturity and victory because they are trying to become something they already are.

You Were Baptized into Christ's Death

"Don't you know that all of us who were baptized into Christ Jesus were baptized into his death?" (Romans 6:3). You may still be wondering, "How do I do that?" The answer is the same: You can't do it, because you have already been baptized into Christ Jesus. It happened the moment you placed your faith in Jesus Christ as Savior and Lord. It is futile to seek something which the Bible affirms we already have: "We were all baptized by one Spirit into one body" (1 Corinthians 12:13). "We were" is past tense. It's done, so it must be believed.

The ordinance of water baptism is understood by most Christians to be the symbolic representation of what has already been done. Augustine called baptism a visible form of an invisible grace. It is a public identification with the death, burial, and resurrection of the Lord

Jesus Christ. Those who practice infant baptism understand the ordinance to identify with the Holy Spirit
coming upon Christ. They sprinkle water on the infant's
head instead of immersing the body. Both look to Scripture for the basis of their practice, and both see it as an
identification with Christ. The passage we are looking at,
however, deals with our spiritual baptism into Christ, of
which the external ordinance practiced by most of our
churches is a symbol.

When Christ died on the cross and was buried, as
pictured by a baptismal candidate being immersed in
water, you died and were buried to sin. And when you
placed your faith in Jesus Christ as Savior and Lord, your
death and burial was activated. You died then; you can't
do it again. You can only believe it.

You Were Raised to New Life in Christ

"We were therefore buried with him through baptism
into death in order that, just as Christ was raised from the
dead through the glory of the Father, we too may live a
new life. If we have been united with him like this in his
death, we will certainly also be united with him in his
resurrection" (Romans 6:4,5). Have we been united with
Him? Absolutely! "If we have been united with him" is
described by those who study the original languages as a
first class conditional clause. It can literally be read: "If
we have become united with Him in the likeness of His
death—and we certainly have—we shall also be united
with him in the likeness of His resurrection."

Paul's argument in this passage is twofold. First, you
cannot have only part of Jesus. You cannot identify with
the death and burial of Christ without also identifying
with His resurrection and ascension. You will live in

defeat if you believe only half the gospel. You have died with Christ, *and* you have been raised with Him and seated in the heavenlies (Ephesians 2:6). From this position you have the authority and power you need to live the Christian life.

Every child of God is spiritually alive and therefore "in Christ." Paul clearly identifies every believer with Christ:

In His death	Romans 6:3,6; Galatians 2:20; Colossians 3:1-3
In His burial	Romans 6:4
In His resurrection	Romans 6:5,8,11
In His ascension	Ephesians 2:6
In His life	Romans 5:10,11
In His power	Ephesians 1:19,20
In His inheritance	Romans 8:16,17; Ephesians 1:11,12

The second part of Paul's argument is that death no longer has any power over you, and therefore neither does sin. We will see how and why this is true when we get to those verses.

Jesus didn't come only to die for our sins; He also came that we might have life (John 10:10). We celebrate the resurrection of Jesus Christ on Easter, not just His death on Good Friday. It is the resurrected life of Christ that God has given to us.

Notice how Paul develops this truth in Romans 5:8-11. "God demonstrates his own love for us in this·

While we were still sinners, Christ died for us" (verse 8). Isn't that great, Christian? God loves you! But is that all? No! "Since we have now been justified by his blood, how much more shall we be saved from God's wrath through him!" (verse 9).

Isn't that great, Christian? You're not going to hell! But is that all? No! "For if, when we were God's enemies, we were reconciled to him through the death of his Son, how much more, having been reconciled, shall we be saved through his life!" (verse 10).

Isn't that great, Christian? You have been saved by His life. Eternal life isn't something you get when you die. You are alive in Christ right now. But is that all? No! "Not only is this so, but we also rejoice in God through our Lord Jesus Christ, through whom we have now received reconciliation" (verse 11). This reconciliation assures us that our souls are in union with God, which is what it means to be spiritually alive.

Peter also affirms this incredible truth: "His divine power has given us everything we need for life and godliness through our knowledge of him who called us by his own glory and goodness. Through these he has given us his very great and precious promises, so that through them you may participate in the divine nature and escape the corruption in the world caused by evil desires" (2 Peter 1:3,4). Are you beginning to see a glimmer of hope for overcoming sexual bondage? You should be, because you have already died to it and been raised to new and victorious life in Christ.

Your Old Self Was Crucified with Christ

"For we know that our old self was crucified with him so that the body of sin might be done away with, that we should no longer be slaves to sin" (Romans 6:6). The text does not say "we do" but "we know." Your old self was crucified when Christ was crucified. The only proper response to this marvelous truth is to believe it. Many people are desperately trying to put to death the old self with all its tendencies to sin, but they can't do it. Why not? Because it is already dead! You cannot do what God alone can and has already done for you.

Christians who continually fail in their Christian experience begin to question incorrectly, "What experience must I undergo in order for me to live victoriously?" There is none. The only experience that was necessary for this verse to be true occurred nearly 2000 years ago on the cross. And the only way we can enter into that experience today is by faith. We can't save ourselves, and we can't by human effort overcome the penalty of death or the power of sin. Only God can do that for us, and He has already done it.

As I was explaining this truth during a conference, a man raised his hand and said, "I've been a Christian for 13 years. Why hasn't someone told me this before?" Maybe no one shared with him, or maybe he wasn't listening. Some have asserted that this is just "positional truth," implying that there is little or no present-day benefit for being in Christ. What a tragic conclusion! This is not pie-in-the-sky theology. There is a powerful application of this truth to daily life. If we choose to believe it and walk accordingly by faith, the truth of this passage works out in our experience. Trying to make it true by our experience will only lead to defeat.

We don't live obediently hoping that God may someday accept us. We are already accepted by God, so we live obediently. We don't labor in God's vineyard hoping that He may someday love us. God already loves us, so we joyfully labor in His vineyard. It is not what we do that determines who we are; it is who we are and what we believe that determines what we do.

You Have Been Freed from Sin

"Anyone who has died has been freed from sin" (Romans 6:7). Have you died with Christ? Then you are free from sin. You may be thinking, "I don't feel free from sin." If you only believe what you feel, you will never live a victorious life. In all honesty, I wake up quite a few mornings and feel very alive to sin and dead to Christ. But that's just the way I feel. If I believed what I feel and walked that way the rest of my day, what kind of a day do you think I would have? It would be a pretty bad day!

Rather, I have learned to get up in the morning and say, "Thank You, Lord, for another day. I deserved eternal damnation, but You gave me eternal life. I ask You to fill me with Your Holy Spirit, and I choose to walk by faith regardless of how I feel. I realize that I will face many temptations today, but I choose to take every thought captive to the obedience of Christ and to think upon that which is true and right."

One seminary student heard me teaching this concept and responded, "Are you telling me I don't have to sin?"

I said, "Where did you ever get the idea that you have to sin?" Then I read 1 John 2:1 to him: "My dear children, I write this to you so that you will not sin. But if anybody does sin, we have one who speaks to the Father in our defense—Jesus Christ, the Righteous One." God does not refer to us in Scripture as sinners but saints who can choose to sin. Obviously, Christian maturity is a factor in our ability to stand against temptation. But what an incredible sense of defeat must accompany the belief that we are bound to sin when God commands us not to sin! Many people in sexual bondage are caught in this hopeless web. They think, "God, You made me this way, and now You condemn me for it. Unfair!"

Others say, "The Christian life is impossible." Then when they fail, they proclaim, "I'm only human!" Those who struggle with sexual sins lead the parade in this category. They believe the lie that the gospel isn't big enough to cover sexual bondage. This attitude reflects a faulty belief system. We have been saved, not by how we *behave*, but how we *believe*. This is a paradox and often a stumbling block to the natural mind. But to biblically informed Christians it is the basis for our freedom and conquest—our union with God and our walk by faith.

There is no greater sin than the sin of unbelief. On more than one occasion the Lord made statements like, "According to your faith will it be done to you" (Matthew 9:29). Paul wrote, "Everything that does not come from faith is sin" (Romans 14:23). If we choose to believe a lie, we will live a lie, but if we choose to believe the truth, we will live a victorious life by faith in the same way that we were saved.

Death Is No Longer Your Master

"If we died with Christ, we believe that we will also live with him. For we know that since Christ was raised from the dead, he cannot die again; death no longer has mastery over him" (Romans 6:8,9). Does death have mastery over you? Absolutely not! Why? Because death could not master Christ, and you are in Him. " 'Death has been swallowed up in victory.' 'Where, O death, is your victory? Where, O death, is your sting?' The sting of death is sin, and power of sin is the law. But thanks be to God! He gives us the victory through our Lord Jesus Christ" (1 Corinthians 15:54-57).

Since Christ has triumphed over death by His resurrection, death has no mastery over us who are spiritually alive in Christ Jesus. Jesus said, "I am the resurrection and the life. He who believes in me will live [spiritually], even though he dies [physically]; and whoever lives and believes in me will never die [spiritually]. Do you believe this?" (John 11:25,26). Do you believe? Be it done to you according to how you believe!

Sin Is No Longer Your Master

Paul argues that if death has no mastery over us, then neither does sin. "The death he died, he died to sin once for all; but the life he lives, he lives to God" (Romans 6:10). This was accomplished when "God made him who had no sin to be sin for us, so that in him we might become the righteousness of God" (2 Corinthians 5:21). When Jesus went to the cross, all the sins of the world were upon Him. When they nailed those spikes into His hands and feet, all the sins of the world were upon Him. But when He was resurrected, there were no sins upon Him. They stayed in the grave. As He sits at the right hand of the Father today, there are no sins upon Him. He has triumphed over sin and death. And since you are in Him, you are also dead to sin.

Many Christians accept the truth that Christ died for the sins they have already committed. But what about the sins they commit in the future? When Christ died for all your sins, how many of your sins were then future? All of them, of course! This is not a license to sin, which leads to bondage, but a marvelous truth on which to stand against

Satan's accusations. It is something we must know in order to live free in Christ.

You Are Dead to Sin and Alive in Christ

How are we to respond to what Christ has accomplished for us by His death and resurrection? Paul summarizes it in Romans 6:11: "In the same way, count yourselves dead to sin but alive to God in Christ Jesus." We do not make ourselves dead to sin by considering it to be so. We consider ourselves dead to sin because God says it is already so. The old King James Version reads, "Reckon yourselves to be dead unto sin." If you think that your reckoning makes you dead to sin, you will reckon yourself into a wreck! We can't make ourselves dead to sin; only God can do that—and He has already done it. Paul is saying that we must keep on choosing to believe by faith what God says is true even when our feelings scream the opposite.

The verb "consider" is present tense. In other words, we must continuously believe this truth, daily affirming that we are dead to sin and alive in Christ. This activity is parallel to abiding in Christ (John 15:1-8) and walking by the Spirit (Galatians 5:16). As we take our stand in the truth of what God has done and who we are in Christ, we will not easily be deceived or carry out the desires of the flesh.

Has sin disappeared because we have died to it? No. Has the power of sin diminished? No, it is still strong and still appealing. But when sin makes its appeal, we have the power to say no to it because our relationship with sin ended when the Lord "rescued us from the dominion of darkness and brought us into the kingdom of the Son he loves" (Colossians 1:13). Paul explains how this is possible in Romans 8:1,2: "Therefore, there is now no condemnation for those who are in Christ Jesus, because through Christ Jesus the law of the Spirit of life set me free from the law of sin and death."

Is the law of sin and death still operative? Yes, because it is a law. But it has been overcome by a greater law—the law of the Spirit of life. It's like flying. Can you fly by our own power? No, because the law of gravity keeps you bound to earth. But you *can* fly if you buy an airline ticket and apply a law greater than gravity: jet propulsion. As long as you stay in that airplane and operate according to the greater law, you will soar. But if you cease to operate under that law by stepping out the door in mid-flight, the law of gravity will quickly take effect and down you will go!

Like gravity, the law of sin and death is still here, still operative, still powerful, and still making its appeal. But you don't need to submit to it. The law of the Spirit of life is a greater law. As long as you live by the Spirit, you will not carry out the desires of the flesh (Galatians 5:16). You must "be strong in the Lord and in his mighty power" (Ephesians 6:10). The moment you think you can stand on your own, the moment you stop depending on the Lord, you are headed for a fall (Proverbs 16:18).

All temptation is an attempt by the devil to get us to live our lives independently of God. "So, if you think you are standing firm, be careful that you don't fall! No temptation has seized you except what is common to man. And God is faithful; he will not let you be tempted beyond what you can bear. But when you are tempted, he will also provide a way out so that you can stand up under it" (1 Corinthians 10:12,13). When we succumb to temptation or are deceived by the father of lies, we should quickly repent of our sin, renounce the lies, return to our loving Father—who cleanses us, and resume the walk of faith.

Perhaps you have struggled in defeat against sexual sin and bondage while vainly trying to figure out what you must do to get free. Hopefully the truth of Romans 6:1-11 has blown away the prison doors in your understanding. It's not what you do that sets you free; it's what you believe. God has done everything that needs to be done through the death and resurrection of Jesus Christ. Your vital first step to freedom is to consider it so, affirm it, and stand on it.

Having taken that step, there are some follow-up steps you must take to apply what God has done to your experience with temptation, sin, and bondage. In the next chapter we will begin to look at these steps.

NINE

Behaving Must Follow Believing

In the previous chapter we examined Romans 6:1-11 to discover what God has done for us, how we must accept His provision, and how we must live by faith in accordance with the truth. The key thought is this: It's not what you do that sets you free from sexual bondage, it's what you believe.

However, according to Romans 6:12,13, there is also something we must do in response to what God has already done. But beware: What God calls you to do in verses 12 and 13 will not be effective in your life if you're not believing what God has called you to believe in verses 1-11. It is the truth that sets us free, and believing the truth must precede and determine responsible behavior.

Give Yourself as an Offering

Paul continues his instruction in Romans 6 with a specific assignment for all believers: "Therefore do not let sin reign in your mortal body so that you obey its evil desires" (verse 12). According to this verse, whose responsibility is it not to allow sin to reign in our bodies? Clearly, it is ours as believers. This means we cannot say, "The devil made me do it." God never commands us to do something we cannot do or that the devil can prevent us from doing. In Christ you have died to sin, and the devil can't *make* you do anything. He will tempt you, accuse you, and try to deceive you. But if sin reigns in your body, it is because you allowed it to happen. You are responsible for your own attitudes and actions.

How then do we prevent sin from reigning in our bodies? Paul answers in verse 13: "Do not offer the parts of your body to sin, as instruments of wickedness, but rather offer yourselves to God, as those who have been brought from death to life; and offer the parts of your body to him as instruments of righteousness." Notice that there is one negative action to avoid and two positive actions to practice.

Don't offer your body to sin. We are not to use our eyes, hands, feet, etc. in any way that would serve sin. When you run across a sexually explicit program on TV and linger lustfully to watch it, you are offering your body to sin. When you get inappropriately "touchy-feely" with a coworker of the opposite sex, you are offering your body to sin. When you fantasize sexually about someone other than your spouse and act out your desires through masturbation, you are offering your body to sin. Whenever you choose to offer yourself to sin, you invite sin to rule in your physical body, something God has commanded us not to do.

Offer yourself and your body to God. Notice that Paul makes a distinction between "yourselves" and "the parts of your body." What is the distinction? Self is who we are on the inside, the immortal, eternal part of us. Our bodies and their various parts are who we are on the outside, the mortal, temporal part of us. Someday we are going to jettison these old earth suits. At that time we will be absent from our mortal bodies and present with the Lord in immortal bodies (2 Corinthians 5:8). As long as we are on planet Earth, however, our inner selves are united with our outer physical bodies. We are to offer the complete package—body, soul, and spirit—to God.

Paul wrote, "The body that is sown is perishable, it is raised imperishable; it is sown in dishonor, it is raised in glory; it is sown in weakness, it is raised in power; it is sown a natural body, it is raised a spiritual body" (1 Corinthians 15:42-44). Our inner man will live forever with our heavenly Father, but our bodies won't. Paul continues, "Flesh and blood cannot inherit the kingdom of God, nor does the perishable inherit the imperishable" (verse 50). That which is mortal is corruptible.

Is our physical body evil? No, it's amoral and neutral. So what are we to do about the neutral disposition of our bodies? We are instructed to present them to God "as instruments of righteousness." To "present" means to place at the disposal of. An instrument can be anything the Lord has entrusted to us, including our bodies. For example, your car is another amoral, neutral instrument for your use. You can use your car for good or bad purposes as you choose to drive people to church or to deliver drugs. Similarly, your body is yours to use for good or evil purposes as you choose. You have opportunities every day to offer your eyes, your hands, your brain, your feet, etc. to sin or to God. The Lord commands us to be good stewards of our bodies and use them only as instruments of righteousness. But ultimately it's our choice.

Your Body, God's Temple

In 1 Corinthians 6:13-20, Paul applies these instructions about the body specifically to the topic of sexual immorality:

> The body is not meant for sexual immorality, but for the Lord, and the Lord for the body. By his power God raised the Lord from the dead, and he will raise us also. Do you not know that your bodies are members of Christ himself? Shall I then take the members of Christ and unite them with a prostitute? Never! Do you not know that he who unites himself with a prostitute is one with her in body? For it is said, "The two will become one flesh." But he who unites himself with the Lord is one with him in spirit.
>
> Flee from sexual immorality. All other sins a man commits are outside his body, but he who sins sexually sins against his own body. Do you not know that your body is a temple of the Holy Spirit, who is in you, whom you have received from God? You are not your own; you were bought at a price. Therefore honor God with your body.

This passage teaches that we have more than a spiritual union with God. Our bodies are members of Christ Himself. Romans 8:11 declares, "If the Spirit of him who raised Jesus from the dead is living in you, he who raised Christ from the dead will also give life to your mortal bodies through his Spirit, who lives in you." Our bodies are actually God's temple, because His Spirit dwells in us. To use our bodies for sexual immorality is to defile the temple of God.

It is hard for us to fully appreciate the moral outrage felt in heaven when one of God's children misuses His temple through sexual sin. It compares to the despicable act of Antiochus Epiphanes in the second century before Christ. This godless Syrian ruler overran Jerusalem, declared Mosaic ceremonies illegal, erected a statue of Zeus in the Temple, and slaughtered a pig—an unclean animal—on the altar. Can you imagine how God's people must have felt to have their holy place so thoroughly desecrated? God must feel the same way when we desecrate His temple—our bodies—through sexual immorality.

As a Christian, aren't you offended when people suggest that Jesus was sexually intimate with Mary Magdalene? This is how God must feel when a member of His pure Son's bride, the church, commits sexual immorality. Jesus was fully God, but He was also fully man. He was tempted in every way we are, including sexually, but He never sinned. His earthly body was not meant for sexual immorality, and neither is ours. If our eyes were fully open to the reality of the spiritual world and we understood the scandal felt in heaven when we sin against our own bodies, we would more quickly obey the Scripture's command to flee from sexual immorality.

Can you think of any way that you could commit a sexual sin and not use your body as an instrument of unrighteousness? I can't. And when we do commit sexual sin, we allow sin to reign in our mortal bodies! Does that mean we are still united with the Lord? Yes, because He will never leave us nor forsake us. We don't lose our salvation, but we certainly lose a degree of freedom. Paul urged, "You were called to freedom, brethren; only do not turn your freedom into an opportunity for the flesh, but through love serve one another" (Galatians 5:13 NASB).

What happens when a child of God who is united with the Lord and one spirit with Him also "unites himself with a prostitute" through sexual immorality? The Bible says he becomes one flesh with the object of his sin. Somehow they bond together. Bonding is a positive thing in a wholesome relationship, but in an immoral union bonding only leads to bondage.

How many times have you heard of a nice Christian young woman who becomes involved with an immoral man, has sex with him, and then continues in a sick relationship for two or three years? He takes advantage of her and abuses her. Friends and relatives tell her, "He's no good for you." But she won't listen to them. Even though her boyfriend treats her badly, the girl won't leave him. Why? Because a spiritual and emotional bond has formed. They have become one flesh. Such bonds must be broken. That's one reason why God instructs us not to become entangled in immoral activities and relationships in the first place.

This spiritual and emotional bond can occur even as a result of heavy petting. At one of my conferences, a colleague and I counseled a young husband and wife who were experiencing marital problems. Even though they were deeply committed to each other and highly respected each other, their sexual relationship had been lifeless and dull since their wedding. Both husband and wife had been very romantically involved before marriage with other partners, but without intercourse.

During our counseling session, both husband and wife admitted for the first time that they were still emotionally attached to their "first loves." At our encouragement, they renounced petting and romantic involvement with their previous partners and recommitted their lives and their bodies to the Lord. They further committed to reserve the sexual use of their bodies for each other only. The next day they shared with me that they had a joyful, intimate encounter with each other that night—a first for their marriage. Once the sexual bonds were broken, they were free to enjoy each other the way God intended.

The Beauty of Offering Yourself to God

Wonderful things happen when we determine to offer our bodies to God as instruments of righteousness instead of offering our bodies to sin. The Bible's sacrificial system provides a beautiful illustration.

The sin offering in the Old Testament was a blood offering. Blood was drained from the sacrificial animal, and the carcass was taken outside the camp and disposed of. Only the blood was offered to God for the forgiveness of sin. Hebrews 9:22 states, "Without the shedding of blood there is no forgiveness."

At the cross, the Lord Jesus Christ became our sin offering. After He shed His blood for us, His body was taken down and buried outside the city, but unlike the slain lamb of the Old Testament, the Lamb of God did not stay buried for long.

There was also a burnt offering in the Old Testament. Unlike the sin offering which involved only blood, the burnt offering was totally consumed on the altar—blood, carcass, everything. In the Hebrew, "burnt" literally means "that which ascends." In the burnt offering, the whole sacrificial animal ascended to God in flames and smoke from the altar. It was "an aroma pleasing to the Lord" (Leviticus 1:9).

Jesus is the sin offering, but who is the burnt offering? We are! Paul writes, "I urge you, brothers, in view of God's mercy, to offer your bodies as living sacrifices, holy and pleasing to God—this is your spiritual act of worship" (Romans 12:1). It's wonderful that our sins are forgiven; Christ did that for us when He shed His blood. But if you want to live victoriously in Christ over the lust and sin which plagues you, you must present yourself to God and your body as an instrument of righteousness. Such a sacrifice is "pleasing to God" as the aroma of the burnt offering was in the Old Testament.

A tremendous spiritual revival under King Hezekiah is recorded in 2 Chronicles 29. First, he cleaned out the temple and prepared it for worship by purifying it. What a beautiful picture of repentance from past sins! Then he ordered the blood offering for the forgiveness of sins. Nothing really extraordinary happened during the blood offering, but according to God's law, the sins of the people were forgiven. Then "Hezekiah gave the order to sacrifice the burnt offering on the altar. As the offering began, singing to the Lord began also. . . . All this continued until the sacrifice of the burnt offering was completed" (2 Chronicles 29:27,28). The burnt offering was such a significant and worshipful event that it was surrounded by music. The account concludes, "Hezekiah and all the people rejoiced at what God had brought about for his people" (verse 36). Great joy results when believers obediently and wholeheartedly present themselves to God.

Ephesians 5:18-20 gives us a similar picture of the beauty of offering ourselves completely to God. "Do not get drunk on wine, which leads to debauchery. Instead, be filled with the Spirit" (verse 18). In other words, don't defile the temple of God, but let the Spirit of God rule in your hearts. Guess what happens when you do? You will be prepared to fulfill verses 19,20: "Speak to one another with psalms, hymns, and spiritual songs. Sing and make music in your heart to the Lord, always giving thanks to God the Father for everything." Music fills the temple when we yield ourselves to God.

Winning the Struggle with Sin

Sadly, the music ringing inside many Christians today is more of a funeral dirge than a song of joy. They feel defeated instead of victorious. They have offered their bodies as instruments of sexual sin and feel hopelessly trapped in sexual bondage. They may experience occasional periods of relief and success at saying no to temptation. But since sin has been allowed to reign in their bodies, they continue to crash in defeat. Perhaps you find yourself in this discouraging condition.

Paul clearly describes this struggle and its solution in Romans 7:15-25. The discussion which follows is based on many counseling sessions I have had with Christians struggling with temptation, sin, and bondage, including the sexual arena. You may find yourself identifying with Dan as I talk through Romans 7:15-25 (NASB) with him. I trust you will also identify with the liberating truth of God's Word.[1]

> *Dan:* Neil, I can't keep going on like this. I have been sexually promiscuous in the past, and I'm really sorry about it. I have confessed it to the Lord, but I can't seem to get victory over it. I sincerely commit myself to avoid pornography. But the temptation is overwhelming and I give into it. I don't want to live like this! It's ruining my marriage.

Neil: Dan, let's look at a passage of Scripture that seems to describe what you are experiencing. Romans 7:15 reads: "That which I am doing, I do not understand; for I am not practicing what I would like to do, but I am doing the very thing I hate." Would you say that pretty well describes your life?

Dan: Exactly! I really desire to do what God says is right, and I hate being in bondage to this lust. I sneak down at night and call one of those sex hotlines. Afterward I feel disgusted with myself.

Neil: It sounds like you would identify with verse 16 as well: "But if I do the very thing I do not wish to do, I agree with the law, confessing that it is good." Dan, how many persons are mentioned in this verse?

Dan: There is only one person, and it is clearly "I."

Neil: It is very defeating when we know what we want to do but for some reason can't do it. How have you tried to resolve this conflict in your own mind?

Dan: Sometimes I wonder if I'm even a Christian. It seems to work for others, but not for me. I sometimes question if the Christian life is possible or if God is really here.

Neil: You're not alone, Dan. Many Christians believe that they are different from others, and most think they are the only ones who struggle with sexual temptations. If you were the only player in this battle, it would stand to reason that you would question your salvation or the existence of God.

But look at verse 17: "So now, no longer am I the one doing it, but sin which indwells me." Now how many players are there?

Dan: Apparently two, "I" and "sin." But I don't understand.

Neil: Let's read verse 18 and see if we can make some sense out of it: "I know that nothing good dwells in me, that is, in my flesh; for the wishing is present in me, but the doing of the good is not."

Dan: I learned that verse a long time ago. It has been easy for me to accept that I'm no good for myself and no good for my wife. Sometimes I think it would be better if I just wasn't here.

Neil: That's not true, because that's not what the verse says. In fact it says the opposite. The "nothing good" that is dwelling in you is not you. It's something else. If I had a wood splinter in my finger it would be "nothing good" dwelling in me. But the "nothing good" isn't me; it's a splinter. It is important to note that the "nothing good" is not even my flesh, but it dwells in my flesh. If we see only ourselves in this struggle, living righteously will seem hopeless. These passages are going to great lengths to tell us that there is a second party involved in our struggle whose nature is evil and different from ours.

You see, Dan, when you and I were born, we were born under the penalty of sin. And we know that Satan and his emissaries are always working to keep us under that penalty. When God saved us, Satan lost that battle, but he didn't curl up his tail or pull in his fangs. He is now committed to keeping us under the power of sin. But in Christ we have died to sin and are no longer under its power.

In 1 John 2:12-14, John writes to little children because their sins are forgiven. In other words, they have overcome the penalty of sin. He writes to young men because they have overcome the evil one. In other words, they have overcome the power of sin. We have the authority in Christ to overcome the penalty and power of sin despite Satan's lies that we are still under them. The passage we are looking at also says that this evil is going to work through the flesh, which remained with us after our salvation. It is our responsibility to crucify the flesh and to resist the devil.

Let's continue in the passage to see if we can learn more about how the battle is being waged. Verses 19-21 state: "For the good that I wish, I do not do; but I practice the very evil that I do not wish. But if I am doing the very thing I do not wish, I am no longer the one doing it, but sin which dwells in me. I find then the principle that evil is present in me, the one who wishes to do good."

Dan: Sure, it is clearly evil and sin. But isn't it just my own sin? When I sin, I feel guilty.

Neil: There's no question that you and I sin, but we are not "sin" as such. Evil is present in us, but we are not evil per se. This does not excuse us from sinning, because Paul wrote in Romans 6:12 that we are responsible not to let sin reign in our mortal bodies. When you came under conviction about your sexual sin, what did you do?

Dan: I confessed it to God.

Neil: Dan, confession literally means to agree with God. It is the same thing as walking in the light or living in moral agreement with Him about our present condition. We must confess our sin if we are going to live in harmony with our heavenly Father, but it doesn't go far enough. Confession is only the first step to repentance. The man that Paul is writing about agrees with God that what he is doing is wrong, but it didn't resolve his problem. You have confessed your sin to God, but you are still in bondage to lust. It has to be very frustrating for you. Have you ever felt so defeated that you just want to lash out at someone or yourself?

Dan: Almost every day!

Neil: But when you cool down, do you again entertain thoughts that are in line with who you really are as a child of God?

Dan: Always, and then I feel terrible about lashing out.

Neil: Verse 22 explains why: "For I joyfully concur with the law of God in the inner man." When we act out of character with who we really are, the Holy Spirit immediately brings conviction because of our union with God. Out of frustration and failure we think or say things like, "I'm not going back to church anymore. Christianity doesn't work. It was God who made me this way, and now I feel condemned all the time. God promised to provide a way of escape. Well, where is it? I haven't found it!" But soon our true nature begins to express itself. "I know what I'm doing is wrong, and I know God loves me, but I'm so frustrated by my continuing failure."

Dan: Someone told me once that this passage was talking about a non-Christian.

Neil: I know some good people who take that position, but that doesn't make sense to me. Does a natural man joyfully concur with the law of God in the inner man? Does an unbeliever agree with the law of God and confess that it is good? I don't think so! In fact, they speak out rather strongly against it. Some even hate us Christians for upholding such a moral standard.

Now look at verse 23, which describes the nature of this battle with sin: "But I see a different law in the members of my body, waging war against the law of my mind, and making me a prisoner of the law of sin which is in my members." According to this passage, Dan, where is the battle being fought?

Dan: The battle appears to be in the mind.

Neil: That's precisely where the battle rages. Now if Satan can get you to think you are the only one in the battle, you will get down on yourself or God when you sin, which is counterproductive to resolving the problem. Let me put it this way: Suppose you opened a door that you were told not to open, and a dog came through the door and wrapped his teeth around your leg. Would you beat on yourself or would you beat on the dog?

Dan: I suppose I would beat on the dog.

Neil: Of course you would. On the other side of the door, another dog—Satan—is tempting you with thoughts like, "Come on, open the door. I have an exciting video to show you. Everybody else is doing it. You'll get away with it." So you open the door and the dog comes in and grabs hold of your leg. You feel the pain of conviction and the sting of sin. Then the tempter switches to being the accuser. Your mind is pummeled with his accusations: "You opened the door. You're a miserable excuse for a Christian. God certainly can't love someone as sinful as you."

So you cry out, "God, forgive me!" And He does. But the dog is still clinging to your leg! You go through the cycle repeatedly: sin, confess, sin, confess, sin, confess. You beat on yourself continuously for your repeated failure.

People get tired of beating on themselves, so they walk away from God under a cloud of defeat and condemnation. Paul expressed this feeling in verse 24: "Wretched man that I am! Who will set me free from the body of this death?" He doesn't say he's wicked or sinful, but that he's miserable. This man is not free. His attempts to do the right thing are met in moral failure because he has submitted to God but has not resisted the devil (James 4:7). There is nobody more miserable than someone who knows what is right and wants to do what is right but can't.

Dan: That's me—miserable!

Neil: Wait a minute, Dan. There is victory. Jesus will set us free. Look at verse 25: "Thanks be to

God through Jesus Christ our Lord! So then, on the one hand I myself with my mind am serving the law of God, but on the other, with my flesh the law of sin." Let's go back to the dog illustration. Why isn't crying out to God enough to solve your ongoing conflict with sexual sin?

Dan: Well, like you said, the dog is still there. I guess I have to chase off the dog.

Neil: You will also have to close the door. What have you done to resolve your sexual sins and temptations?

Dan: Like I said, I have confessed them to God and asked His forgiveness.

Neil: But as you have already found out, that didn't quite resolve the problem. Here are the steps you must take.

First, realize that you are already forgiven. Christ died once for all your sins. You were right in confessing your sin to God, because you need to own up to the fact that you opened the door when you knew it was wrong.

Second, to make sure that every door is closed, you need to ask the Lord to reveal to your mind every sexual use of your body as an instrument of unrighteousness. As the Lord brings them to your mind, renounce them. Your body belongs to God and it is not to be used for sexual immorality.

Third, present your body to God as a living sacrifice and reserve the sexual use of your body for your spouse only.

Finally, resist the devil and he will flee from you.

Dan: I think I'm getting the picture. But every sexual use of my body! That will take a long time. But even if it took a couple of hours, I guess it would be a lot easier than living in bondage for the rest of my life. I've been condemning myself for my inability to live the Christian life. I can also see why I have been questioning my salvation. I see that Paul was frustrated about his failure, but he didn't get down on himself. He accepts his responsibility. More important, he expresses confidence by turning to God, because the Lord Jesus Christ will enable him to live above sin.

Neil: You're on the right track. Condemning yourself won't help because there is no condemnation for those who are in Christ Jesus (Romans 8:1). We don't want to assist the devil in his role as the accuser. Most people who are in bondage question their salvation. I have counseled hundreds who have shared with me their doubts about God and themselves. Ironically, the very fact that they are sick about their sin and want to get out of it is one of the biggest assurances of their salvation. Non-Christians don't have those kind of convictions.

Romans 7:15-25 contains truth you must believe about sin and Satan and implies steps of action you must take to resist him. There is one more important thing you need to know: No one particular sin, including sexual sin, is isolated from the rest of reality. To gain complete freedom, you need to walk through all the Steps to Freedom in Christ (see Appendix A).

In further preparation for doing so, you also need to understand the battle which is raging for your mind. Satan is a defeated foe, but if he can get you to believe a lie, he can control your life. In the next chapter we will seek to understand how our minds function so that we can win this critical battle.

TEN

Rethink How You Think

Imagine that you have worked most of your adult life for the same boss, a cantankerous, unreasonable tyrant. The man is known throughout the company for bursting into employees' offices and chewing them out royally for even the slightest suspicion of a mistake. You learned early during your employment to walk on eggshells around the old grouch and avoid him as much as possible. Every time he appears at your door you automatically cringe in fear, expecting to get blasted, even if he has only come to borrow a paper clip.

One day you arrive at work to learn that the boss has been suddenly transferred to another branch. You are no longer under his authority, and your relationship with him has ended. Your new boss is a saint—mild-mannered, kind, considerate, affirming. He clearly has the best interests of his employees at heart. But how do you think you will behave around him? Whenever you see your new boss coming down the hall, you start looking for a place to hide, just like you did around the old boss. Whenever the man steps into your office, your heart jumps into your throat. You wonder what you're going to get reamed out for this time. The more you get to know your new boss the more you realize he is as different from your old boss as night is from day. But it will take time to get to know your new boss and to change the negative reaction you learned under the old authority in your life.

Old habits are hard to break. Once we become conditioned to a certain stimulus-response pattern, it can be difficult to reprogram our minds. This is certainly true of established sexual thought patterns and habits which are contrary to God's Word, patterns which may have been ingrained in us long before we became Christians.

We learned from Romans 6:1-11 that we are no longer under the authority of sin and Satan, because our relationship with them has been severed. We are new creatures in Christ (2 Corinthians 5:17). Old thought patterns and habits of responding to temptations don't automatically go away. They are still with us. Some traumatic memories of abuse during childhood still cause us to recoil in pain after all these years. We have a new boss—Jesus Christ, but having lived under the domination of sin and Satan, we must adjust to the glorious freedom our new boss has provided for us.

How does that happen? Paul called the process *renewing our minds*. Having instructed us on what to believe about our relationship to sin and Satan (Romans 6:1-11) and challenging us to present ourselves and our bodies to God instead of to sin (Romans 6:12,13; 12:1), Paul urges, "Do not conform any longer to the pattern of this world, but be transformed by the renewing of your mind. Then you will be able to test and approve what God's will is—his good, pleasing and perfect will" (Romans 12:2). Next to what you believe about your relationship to sin, the two most critical issues you face in overcoming sexual bondage are presenting your physical body to God and renewing your mind to line up with God's truth.

Why is renewing the mind so critical? Because no one can consistently live in a way that is inconsistent with how he thinks or perceives himself. What we do doesn't determine who we are; who we are determines what we do. If you continue to think and respond as if you are under the dominion of your old boss, you will continue to live that way. You must change your thinking if you're going to change your behaving.

Reprogramming the Computer

Why do we need to have our minds renewed? Let's answer that question with a brief review of our spiritual history.

Because of the fall of Adam, we are all born physically alive but spiritually dead in our trespasses and sins (Ephesians 2:1). Before we placed faith in Jesus Christ, we had neither the presence of God in our lives nor the knowledge of God's ways. So during those formative years we learned how to live our lives independently of God and gratify our sinful desires. We had no other choice.

Then one day we heard the gospel and decided to invite Jesus into our lives. We were born again. We became new creations in Christ. But unfortunately, there is no erase feature in this tremendous computer we call our mind. Everything that was previously programmed into our memory banks before Christ is still there. Our brains recorded every experience we ever had, good and bad. We remember every sexual temptation and have stored away how gratifying it felt to yield to them. If we don't reprogram our minds we will continue to respond to stimuli the way we learned to under our old boss, Satan.

The good news—literally, the gospel—is that we have at our disposal all the resources we need to renew our minds. The Lord has sent us the Holy Spirit, who is the Spirit of truth (John 14:16,17), and He will guide us into all truth (John 16:13). Because we are in Christ, "we have the mind of Christ" (1 Corinthians 2:16). We have superior weapons to win the battle for our minds. Paul wrote, "For though we live in the world, we do not wage war as the world does. The weapons we fight with are not the weapons of the world. On the contrary, they have divine power to demolish strongholds. We demolish arguments and every pretension that sets itself up against the knowledge of God, and we take captive every thought to make it obedient to Christ" (2 Corinthians 10:3-5). Paul is not talking about defensive armor, but about battering-ram weaponry that tears down strongholds in our minds which have been raised up against the knowledge of God.

Practice Threshold Thinking

If we are going to take the way of escape from sexual bondage that God has provided for us, we must avail ourselves of God's provision and change how we respond at the threshold of every sexual temptation. We must take those first thoughts captive and make them obedient to Christ. If we allow ourselves to ruminate on tempting thoughts, we will eventually act on them.

For example, suppose a man struggles with lust. One night his wife asks him to go to the store for milk. When he gets into the car, he wonders which store he should go to. He remembers that the local convenience store has a display of pornographic magazines within easy reach. He can buy milk at other stores which don't sell those magazines. But the memory of the seductive photos he has ogled before at the convenience store gives rise to a tempting thought. The more he thinks about it, the harder it is to resist. When he pulls out of the driveway, guess which way he turns.

On the way to the convenience store, all kinds of thoughts cross the man's mind. He prays, "Lord, if You don't want me to look at the pornography, have my pastor be in the store buying milk or cause the store to be closed." Since the store is open (do you know any convenience stores that ever close?!) and since the pastor isn't there, he decides it must be okay to take a look. The mind has an incredible propensity to rationalize, which is why tempting thoughts must be arrested before your mind can come up with a reason to act on them.

But the man's stolen pleasure doesn't last. Before he leaves the store, guilt and shame overwhelm him. "Why did I do it?" he moans. He did it primarily because he ignored the way of escape available to him before he even pulled out of the garage. He failed to take that initial thought captive and make it obedient to Christ. Rare is the person who can turn away from sin once the initial tempting thought has been embraced.

Hardware and Software

Why does our mind work this way? To answer this question we need to understand how our outer self—our physical body—relates to our inner self—our soul or spirit. Scripture declares that we have an outer self and an inner self (2 Corinthians 4:16). Our brain is part of the outer self. Our mind is a part of the inner self. There is something fundamentally different between our brain and our mind. Our brain is little more than meat. When we die physically our outer self, including our brain, will return to dust. Our inner self will be absent from the body. We will be brainless, but we will not be mindless.

God has obviously created the outer self to correlate with the inner self. The correlation between the mind and the brain is clear. The brain functions much like a digital computer. Neurons operate like little switches that turn on and off. Each neuron has many inputs—called dendrites—and only one output, which channels the neurotransmitters to other dendrites. Millions of these connections make up the computer hardware of our brain.

Our mind is the software. As the brain receives input from the external world through the five senses, the mind compiles, analyzes, and interprets the data and chooses responses based on how the mind has been programmed. Before we came to Christ, our minds were programmed by the world, the flesh, and the devil, and our choices were made without the knowledge of God or the benefit of His presence. When we became Christians nobody pressed the CLEAR button in our minds. We need to be reprogrammed by God's truth. We need our minds renewed.

The Western world tends to assume that mental problems are primarily caused by faulty hardware—the brain. There is no question that organic brain syndrome, Alzheimer's disease, and chemical imbalance can impede our ability to function mentally. The best program (mind) won't work if the computer (brain) is unplugged or in disrepair. However, the Christian's struggle with sin and bondage is not primarily a hardware problem but a software problem. Renewing our mind is the process of reprogramming the software.

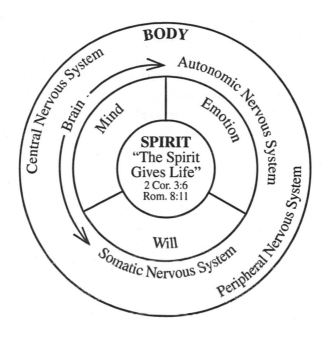

The brain and the spinal cord make up the central nervous system, which splits off into a peripheral nervous system comprised of two channels: the somatic and the autonomic. The somatic system regulates large and small motor movements over which we have volitional control. That's why we can think "move" to an arm, a leg, or a toe, and it moves. The autonomic system regulates organs and glands over which we have no volitional control. We don't have to tell our heart to beat or our glands to secrete. They function automatically, thanks to the autonomic nervous system.

Sex glands are also part of the autonomic nervous system. That's why a woman has no volitional control over her menstrual cycle and a man has no volitional control over erections which occur during sleep. This is just the way God created our outer self to operate.

"But if I have no control over my sex glands," someone may argue, "how can God expect me to control my sexual behavior?" Because self-control is not an action of the outer self but of the inner self. Our sex glands are not the cause of sexual immorality; they just operate based on how the mind is programmed. Sexual behavior is primarily the result of our thought life, and we do have control over what we think. If you fill your mind with pornography, you will drive your autonomic nervous system into the stops. Your sex glands will begin to operate and set in motion behavior you will later regret. You may not have control over what comes out, but you do have control over what you put in. Just like a computer: garbage in, garbage out!

The Power of Visual Stimulation

One of the primary ways we program our mind is through the eye-gate: visual input. Powerful things can happen in just seconds when we see something sexually explicit.

Have you ever wondered why it is so hard to remember some things and forget others? In school we would study all night and then pray that the facts wouldn't leave us before we took the big exam. But just one glance at a pornographic image seems to stay in the mind for years. Why is that?

When we are stimulated emotionally—including being visually stimulated by sexually charged images, an autonomic signal is sent to the adrenal glands. A hormone called epinephrine is secreted into the bloodstream, which locks into the memory whatever stimulus is present at the time of the emotional excitement. This reaction causes us to involuntarily remember emotionally charged events, negative and traumatic ones as well as positive ones. It's too bad we didn't get more emotionally involved with some of our subjects in school; we would have remembered them better!

It has been said that three viewings of hard-core pornography have the same lasting effect on us as the actual illicit experience. A person can become emotionally excited and sexually stimulated just from entertaining thoughts of sexual activity. That's why an aroused man or woman will experience an emotional rush before any sexual contact is made. And that's why a man going to the store where pornography is sold will be sexually stimulated long before he even sees the magazines. It begins in his thoughts, which triggers his autonomic nervous system, which secretes epinephrine into the bloodstream.

The Power of Thoughts over Emotions

Just as we can't control our glands, we can't control our emotions. If you think you can, try liking someone right now that you don't like! We can't order our emotions that way, nor are there any instructions in Scripture to do so. We must acknowledge our emotions, because we can't be right with God if we aren't real about how we feel. But we can't tell ourselves not to feel. What we do have control over is how we think, and how we think controls how we feel. And Scripture does tell us to control our thinking: "Brothers, stop thinking like children. In regard to evil be infants, but in your thinking be adults" (1 Corinthians 14:20).

Incidentally, this verse also reveals why our society's concept of "adults only" is so ridiculous. The phrase implies that there are separate standards of morality for adults and children. Adults are mature enough not to allow their minds to be programmed with filth. Instead the television program announces, "The following content is suitable for 'mature' audiences only. Viewer discretion is advised." The content isn't suitable for anyone, and mature people should be the first to know that. In regard to evil, we should all be like infants: restricting ourselves only to wholesome entertainment. We have already been advised by God concerning sexual immorality in any form: "Flee" (1 Corinthians 6:18).

Since we have no control over how we feel, plan to drop the following line from your repertoire, whether you use it in reference to yourself or to others: "You shouldn't feel that way." That's a subtle form of rejection, because we can't change how we feel. Our feelings are primarily a product of our thought life. What we believe, how we think, and how we perceive ourselves and the world around us determines how we feel. The following story illustrates the point.

Suppose you were paddling a canoe down a beautiful river in the wilderness, enjoying God's creation. As you round a bend in the river, the serenity is disturbed. Standing on the riverbank is someone of the opposite sex. The person is very attractive physically and beckons you to the shore. There is a blanket spread on the riverbank, and your mind and emotions suddenly go wild from the tempting possibilities. Your heart races and your palms are moist. "What an incredible opportunity. We're all alone out here. I can get away with this." Ignoring the conviction, you paddle toward the shore with your emotions up to 9.9 on a scale of 10.

But as you draw nearer the shore, you see an expression of distress instead of seduction on the person's face, and you notice small sores revealing that the person may be suffering from AIDS. You suddenly realize that your initial impression of the stranger was all wrong, and your emotions quickly drop to a .1—from sexual arousal to revulsion, fear, and then compassion for a person in need. You had a totally wrong perception, but your feelings responded to what you believed was the truth. It's clear that the person wasn't beckoning you to the shore for a romantic interlude but calling for help after becoming lost while in such poor health. You quickly confess your wrong thoughts and desires, and then assist the person.

Your first thoughts about that person were wrong, therefore what you felt was a distortion of reality. Our feelings can be distorted by what we choose to think or believe. If what we choose to believe does not reflect truth, then what we feel will not reflect reality. If what we see or mentally visualize is morally wrong, then our emotions are going to be violated. If you want to feel right you must think right.

Choose to Think the Truth

There is someone active in the world today who doesn't want you to think or believe the truth about God, yourself, Christian maturity, or sexual purity. Paul writes, "The Spirit clearly says that in later times some will abandon the faith and follow deceiving spirits and things taught by demons" (1 Timothy 4:1). I have counseled hundreds of people who struggle with their thoughts or literally hear voices. In every case the root problem has been a spiritual battle for their minds. No wonder Paul exhorts us, "Finally, brothers, whatever is true, whatever is noble, whatever is right, whatever is pure, whatever is lovely, whatever is admirable—if anything is excellent or praiseworthy—think about such things" (Philippians 4:8). What joy we would feel if we saw life from God's perspective and entertained only His thoughts!

If Satan can get us to believe a lie, he can control our lives. He is intent on destroying our proper perception of God, ourselves, members of the opposite sex—including our spouses, and the world we live in. Our problems don't just stem from what we believed in the past. Paul says we are to presently and continuously take every thought captive and make it obedient to Christ (2 Corinthians 10:5).

"Thought" is the Greek word *noema*. Notice how Paul uses this word elsewhere in 2 Corinthians. "I have forgiven in the sight of Christ for your sake, in order that Satan might not outwit us. For we are not unaware of his schemes [noema]" (2:10,11). Unforgiveness is a thought that Satan plants in our minds. I believe the greatest access Satan has to the church is our unwillingness to forgive those who have offended us. It certainly has been true with the thousands I have been privileged to work with.

If you have been sexually abused and struggle with thoughts like, "I can't forgive that person," "I hate that person," or "I don't want to forgive him, I want him to suffer as much as he made me suffer," Satan has outwitted you. He has planted his thoughts in your mind. You must renounce those schemes and choose to believe and act on the truth.

Look at another passage in 2 Corinthians: "The god of this age has blinded the minds [noema] of unbelievers, so that they cannot see the light of the gospel of the glory of Christ" (4:4). The one who raises up thoughts against the knowledge of God has a field day with the sexually abused. "Where is your God now?" he taunts. "If God is love, why does He allow the innocent to suffer? If God is all powerful, why didn't He stop that person from violating you?" Such is the smoke screen of lies Satan uses to blind us to the truth.

Look at one more verse: "I am afraid that just as Eve was deceived by the serpent's cunning, your minds [noema] may somehow be led astray from your sincere and pure devotion to Christ" (2 Corinthians 11:3). I'm concerned too, because I see so many people living in bondage to those lies and wandering from devotion to Christ.

Satan is the father of lies, and he will work on our minds to destroy our concept of God and our understanding of who we are as children of God. People in bondage don't know who they are in Christ. That is the one common denominator in every person I have been privileged to help find freedom in Christ. Satan can't do anything about our position in Christ, but if he can get us to believe it isn't true, we will live as though it is not true, even though it is.

Satan preys on the minds of wounded people—the victim of a broken marriage, the child of an alcoholic, someone who was sexually abused as a child, etc. They are prime candidates for Satan's lies because their minds have already been pummeled with self-doubt, fear, anger, and hatred because of their circumstances. But you don't have to be the victim of a broken home or a painful childhood to be the target of the enemy's sexual temptations, accusations, and deceptions.

For example, suppose in a vulnerable moment a young woman has a tempting sexual thought toward someone of the same sex. At first she can't believe she could be tempted to homosexuality. She would probably be embarrassed and immediately flee from the tempting situation.

But she might not tell anyone about it. Who would understand? Then if it happens again and again, she may begin to wonder, "Why am I thinking like this? Could I be one of them?" Once the door of doubt is open, she may begin to seriously question her sexuality.

If her mind continues to dwell on those tempting thoughts, it will affect the way she feels. That's the way God made us—to feel on the basis of how we think. But if she believes what she feels and behaves accordingly, she will use her body as an instrument of unrighteousness. Sin will then reign in her mortal body. Unless she takes those thoughts captive and makes them obedient to Christ, she is on her way to sexual bondage.

Don't assume that all disturbing thoughts are from Satan. We live in a sinful world with tempting images and messages all around us. You have memories of hurtful experiences which prompt thoughts contrary to the knowledge of God. Whether the thought was introduced into your mind from the television set, your memory bank, the pit itself, or your own imagination doesn't matter much, because the answer is always the same: Choose to reject the lie and think the truth.

You can try to analyze the source of every thought, but it won't resolve the problem. Too much of the recovery movement is caught up in the paralysis of analysis. Someone may be able to give a brilliant analysis of what's wrong and still be mired in the problem. The answer is Christ. His truth will set us free.

Breaking the Strongholds

Can strongholds of sexual bondage in the mind be broken? Yes! If our minds have been programmed wrongly, they can be reprogrammed. If we learned something the wrong way, we can learn it the right way. Will this take time? Yes, it will take the rest of our lives to renew our minds and to develop our character. We will never be perfect in our understanding on this earth, nor will our character be perfect like Christ's, but this is what we pursue.

Christian maturity cannot fully take place, however, unless we are free in Christ. When people aren't free in Christ they go from book to book, from pastor to pastor, and from counselor to counselor, but nothing seems to work. Watch how fast they can grow, however, when they are free in Christ!

After I had the privilege of helping a missionary find her freedom in Christ, she wrote, "I'm firmly convinced of the significant benefits of finding our freedom in Christ. I was making some progress in therapy, but there is no comparison with the steps I am able to make now. My ability to 'process' things has increased manyfold. Not only is my spirit more serene, my head is actually clearer! It's easier to make connections now. It seems like everything is easier to understand now."

As we set about demolishing sexual strongholds in our mind, we are not just up against the world—the godless system we were raised in. And we are not just up against the flesh—including those preprogrammed habit patterns of thought that have been burned into our minds over time or by intense traumatic experiences. We're up against the world, the flesh, and the devil. All three influences are at work to turn our minds away from the truth and set us on a path to sexual bondage.

The death and resurrection of Christ dealt a death-blow to Satan's kingdom. But the world system remained after the cross. Television programming, for instance, will never be totally cleaned up. And some of you work where pornography is displayed and people will use the

Lord's name in vain. The world's influence is all around us. As Paul identified himself more with Christ and less with the world, he was able to say, "May I never boast except in the cross of our Lord Jesus Christ, through which the world has been crucified to me, and I to the world" (Galatians 6:14). We must consider ourselves dead to a world system which largely opposes God's truth and sexual purity.

The flesh also remains with the Christian after salvation, but as we bond to Christ we also crucify the flesh. "Those who belong to Christ Jesus have crucified the sinful nature [flesh] with its passions and desires. Since we live by the Spirit, let us keep in step with the Spirit" (Galatians 5:24,25).

Satan still exerts his power in the fallen world. But we are dead to sin and alive in Christ. When we resist the devil he will flee from us (James 4:7).

Cleaning Up the Mind

When I was a young Christian, I decided to clean up my mind. I had a very clean upbringing, for which I am thankful, and became a Christian in my twenties. But after four years in the Navy my mind was cluttered with a lot of junk. I had seen enough pornography to plague me for years. Images would dance in my mind for months after one look. I hated it. I struggled every time I went to a place where pornography was available.

When I made the decision to clean up my mind, do you think the battle got easier or harder? It got harder, of course. Temptation isn't much of a battle if you easily give in to it. But it is fierce when you decide to stand against it. I finally got the victory, however. The following illustration may be helpful as you set out to rid your mind of years of impure thoughts.

Think of your polluted mind as a pot filled to the brim with black coffee. Sitting beside the coffeepot is a huge bowl of crystal-clear ice, which represents the Word of God. Your goal is to purify the contents in the pot by adding ice cubes to it. Every cube displaces some of the coffee and dilutes the rest, making it a little purer. You can only put in one or two cubes a day, so the process seems futile at first. But over the course of time the water begins to look less and less polluted and the taste and smell of coffee is greatly diminished. The process continues to work provided you don't add more coffee grounds.

Paul writes, "Let the peace of Christ rule in your hearts, since as members of one body you were called to peace. And be thankful" (Colossians 3:15). How do we rid ourselves of evil thoughts, purify our mind, and allow the peace of Christ to reign? Shall we focus on rebuking all those tempting, accusing, and deceiving thoughts? If we do, we'll spend the rest of our lives doing nothing more. It would be as futile as trying to separate the coffee from the water after it has percolated.

The answer is found in Colossians 3:16: "Let the word of Christ dwell in you richly." The psalmist gave similar instruction: "How can a young man keep his way pure? By living according to your word. I seek you with all my heart; do not let me stray from your commands. I have hidden your words in my heart that I might not sin against you" (Psalm 119:9-11). Merely trying to stop thinking bad thoughts won't work. We must fill our minds with the crystal-clear Word of God. God has no alternative plan. We are not called to dispel the darkness, we are called to turn on the light. We overcome the father of lies by choosing the truth!

You may find that winning the battle for your mind will initially be a two-steps-forward, one-step-back process as you take on the world, the flesh, and the devil. But gradually it will become three steps forward, one step back, then four and five steps forward as you learn to take every thought captive and make it obedient to Christ. You may despair with all your steps backward, but God won't give up on you. Remember, your sins are already forgiven. You only need to fight for your own personal victory over sin. This is a winnable war because you are alive in Christ and dead to sin. The bigger battle has already been won by Christ.

Freedom to be all that God has called you to be is the greatest blessing in this present life. This freedom is worth fighting for. As you learn more about who you are as a child of God and about the nature of the battle waging for your mind, the process becomes easier. Eventually it is 20 steps forward and one back, and finally the steps are all forward, with only an occasional slip in the battle for the mind.

ELEVEN

Recovery in Christ

Nancy, a devoted wife and mother, attended my conference on resolving personal and spiritual conflicts. During the sessions I related several tremendous stories of persons who had experienced unspeakable atrocities and pain as victims of child abuse and who had found their freedom in Christ. As Nancy listened to the testimonies she felt nauseated, dizzy, and disgusted. Later in the week she confronted me with stern questions: "Why are you telling these awful stories? Those poor children were not at fault. I'm so angry with you. Why are you doing this?"

I wasn't surprised by Nancy's response, because the conference often surfaces in people a lot of problems which haven't been dealt with. So I told her, "These stories are not intended to cause pain; they are stories of victory and hope. I don't think your response has anything to do with me or the testimonies. The Lord is using this conference to bring to the surface something in your life that hasn't been resolved, and the evil one doesn't like it. He's behind your agitation. Please talk with one of our

171

Freedom In Christ staff members, because there is something you need to face and resolve." Indeed there was! Nancy spent the rest of that morning and part of the afternoon finding her freedom in Christ.

Two weeks later Nancy shared her testimony with me, which related to a bedtime story she had often read to her children, *The Bears on Hemlock Mountain.* She recounted how Jonathan, the main character in the short children's story, trudged up the mountain to fetch a large kettle for his mother. On the way he sang, "There are no bears on Hemlock Mountain. No bears. No bears. No bears at all."

He saw dark figures in the distance that looked like bears. But he knew they couldn't be bears, because he didn't want to believe there were bears on Hemlock Mountain. So he continued to climb and sing, "There are no bears on Hemlock Mountain. No bears. No bears. No bears at all." Then he saw a bear. He quickly scrambled under the kettle for safety. He remained hidden until his father and uncles arrived with their guns to rescue him from the bears.

Nancy said that she had been confronted with "dark figures" from her past, but she would not allow her mind to accept the possibility that she had "bears" in her life. It was as if she sang herself to sleep each night, "There was no sexual molestation in my past, no sexual molestation at all." But there were "bear tracks" everywhere. Memories of sexual abuse flooded her mind, but she didn't want to admit it and face the truth. She hid under a kettle of denial.

Finally, during the conference, she understood that she no longer needed to be afraid, because her heavenly Father had overcome the painful threat of the bear of sexual abuse. He had already destroyed the bear, and facing the truth was her only way of escape. After she renounced the unrighteous use of her body and forgave her abuser, there was peace in her life and safety at last on her "Hemlock Mountain."

Perhaps your experience parallels that of Nancy. The truth and testimonies in the previous chapters of this book have brought into sharp focus your shame, failure, and pain in the area of sexual promiscuity, sexual disorientation, or sexual abuse. You may have been in denial for years, insisting, "I don't have a problem." But your lack of peace and victory regarding the sexual sin in your life has worn you down. Try as you might to avoid it, you keep falling into the same thoughts and behaviors again and again. You're too tired to run away anymore. You're ready to take the way of escape from sexual bondage Christ has provided for you.

As I have indicated throughout this book, a key element to finding your freedom in Christ is taking the specific Steps to Freedom in Christ found in Appendix A. In this chapter we will prepare you for that experience.

Take the Initiative

A prerequisite to finding your freedom from sexual bondage is to face the truth, acknowledge the problem, and assume responsibility to change. It's likely that few people know you're in bondage, so you can't count on your family members or friends to urge you into action. Compared to many forms of substance abuse which leave telltale evidence on the body, sexual bondage is relatively easy to hide. For example, someone who is secretly hooked on pornography or illicit sex can lead a Jekyll-and-Hyde existence for many years without being detected. Many people I counsel tell me that they are tired of living a lie.

Nothing will happen until you choose to honestly face your problem and initiate the process for resolving it. God holds each of us responsible for confessing and repenting of our own sin. No one can do that for you.

Inherent in this process is your willingness to submit to God completely without trying to hide anything from Him. Adam and Eve were created to live in a completely transparent relationship with God. They walked with God daily in the garden, naked and unashamed. When they sinned, Adam and Eve covered their nakedness and tried to avoid God. It is ridiculous to try to hide from the all-knowing God. Yet we are often guilty of the same self-deceptive ploy. We mistakenly think that if we go about our daily business, God won't notice that we are hiding in the darkness.

We are spiritually alive in Christ as Adam and Eve were before the fall. God wants us to live before Him "naked and unashamed," completely honest about who we are and what we have done. We must give up our defensive, self-protective posture and determine to walk in the light of His presence.

If we are going to walk as children of light (Ephesians 5:8), we must first understand who we are as children of light. Right belief determines right behavior. If you knew who you were as a child of God, would it affect the way you live? The apostle John sure thought so. "How great is the love the Father has lavished on us, that we should be called children of God! Dear friends, now we are children of God! . . . Everyone who has this hope in him purifies himself, just as he is pure" (1 John 3:1,3). Walking in the light as God's children promises the reward of purity, which perhaps is a quality you have sought in your life for years. You need to know how Christ meets your deepest needs, which is the topic of my book, *Living Free in Christ*. Every chapter describes another facet of who we are in Christ.

Repentance is another aspect of coming clean before God. Repentance means to have a change of mind. It is far more than just mental acknowledgment. It means to turn from our self-centered and self-indulging ways and trust in God. It means no longer to hold iniquity in our hearts. The early church exercised repentance by opening their public profession of faith with the words, "I renounce you, Satan, and all your works and all your ways." The idea is to take back any ground you or your parents or your grandparents have given to Satan.

Repentance involves not only what we turn *from* but what we turn *to*. We must commit all we have and all we are to God. We are to be faithful stewards of everything that God has entrusted to us (1 Corinthians 4:1,2). Such a commitment should include our properties, our ministries, our families, and our physical bodies. As we renounce any previous use of our lives and our possessions in the service of sin and then dedicate ourselves to the Lord, we are saying that the god of this world no longer has any right over us because we now belong to God.

Taking Steps
to Reclaim Your Heritage

The Steps to Freedom in Christ were developed to assist believers in taking back the land that is rightfully theirs. This "land" is our heritage in Christ, the freedom which was purchased on the cross and fully deeded over to us by the resurrected Christ. The Steps to Freedom cover seven critical areas affecting our relationship with God, areas where you may have allowed the prince of darkness to establish strongholds in your life. God has done everything necessary to set us free. It is your responsibility to appropriate what He has done and then to stand firm and resist being lulled back into subjection.

How you view this experience will greatly determine what you gain from it. If you see the Steps simply as a means to rid yourself of bad habits, like employing a counseling technique to move from one life-stage to another, you will receive only limited benefits. There is nothing magical about reading through the steps in Appendix A. The Steps to Freedom in Christ do not set people free; Jesus does. He is the bondage breaker and the way of escape. You will only find your freedom in Him and in response to what He has done. The steps are merely an instrument to help you apply Christ's victory to your need for freedom.

Gearing Up for the Journey

You will find great benefit in going through the Steps in one sitting with a mature Christian friend or leader present to provide accountability and objectivity. Allow plenty of time for the process. It may require many hours to break through the spiritual strongholds which have been erected in your life. When the process is fragmented over two or more appointments, you will miss out on the impact of dealing with each issue in the immediate context of the others, which are often related to the most troublesome area in your life. Furthermore, it may be difficult to bring painful emotions to the surface without resolving them in the same session.

Before going through the steps with your helper, review your personal history with him or her so that specific areas of need can be addressed in the prayers you will pray. The following statements will lead you through the process of sharing your life experiences.

Describe the religious history of your family (parents and grandparents).

Describe your home life from childhood through high school.

Describe your relationship with any adoptive parents, foster parents, or legal guardians.

Discuss any history of physical or emotional illness in your family's background.

Identify any bad eating habits (bulimia, binging and purging, anorexia, compulsive eating, etc.).

Identify any substance addictions (alcohol, drugs).

Identify any prescription drugs you are taking and the reasons for taking them.

Discuss your sleep patterns, problems with insomnia or nightmares, etc.

Discuss any sexual, physical, or emotional abuse you may have suffered.

Identify problems with your thought life (obsessive, blasphemous, condemning, or distracting thoughts in church or during prayer and Bible study; poor concentration; fantasies; etc.).

Describe your general emotional state and any problems you may have with anger, anxiety, depression, bitterness, fear, etc.

Describe your personal spiritual journey (when and how you found Christ, your level of assurance of salvation, etc.).

Not Without a Struggle

As you process through the Steps to Freedom, you may experience feelings of fear or other physical sensations such as heart palpitations, pain in the pit of your stomach, or extreme headaches. These distractions must be acknowledged aloud to God and to the person helping you. The only way you can lose control in this process is if you become distracted and believe a lie. The mind is the battleground, but it is also the control center. It doesn't matter if the thought in your mind is from a speaker on the wall or from the pit. The only way it can have any control over you is if you choose to believe it. Keeping your feelings and fears hidden gives power to the enemy. Getting them into the open and renouncing them breaks his power.

You may experience mental resistance or interference as the steps are being processed. The intensity for some is so great that they want to run out of the room. Others fear that Satan will retaliate when they get home. I regularly hear people say, "This isn't going to work" or "I'm getting a sharp, piercing headache behind my eyes" or "I'm going to throw up." Profane or obscene language may flood the mind. The "f-word" seems to be Satan's favorite. These thoughts and feelings are Satan's schemes to distract you from resolving the conflicts in your life.

To counteract these attacks, I often tell the person I'm helping, "Thank you for letting me know what's happening. I will certainly not force you to go beyond what you think is safe. You have the freedom to leave, but would you be willing to check if this is from the enemy or not? Why don't you again affirm that you are God's child. Then, as His child, commit yourself and your body to Him as a living sacrifice, and by the authority of Christ command Satan and all his evil workers to leave your presence." This simple truth of submitting to God and resisting the devil is effective (James 4:7). When people realize the nature of the battle and where those lies are coming from, they usually respond, "I want to keep going so I can finish this!"

If the feelings or physical sensations persist, ask God to reveal the causes behind them. You may be on the edge of a painful memory that Satan doesn't want you to deal with. Ask God to show you what else you need to do to overcome Satan and to find your freedom. As God brings something to mind, address it openly and deal with it.

If it's a sin, confess it and renounce it. God did not bring it up to badger you, shame you, or condemn you. He is your loving heavenly Father. He is *for* you in this process, not *against* you. Call on Him to help you navigate through the enemy's opposition. He will answer!

If you are being harassed by negative feelings, look for the lie behind them and expose it by declaring the truth. Condemning feelings are almost always the product of false beliefs based on lies. We must learn to recognize these lies and reject them, and then reaffirm and declare the truth of being in Christ. The feelings are real, but when they are lined up with the truth, the lies behind them are exposed. Knowing the truth sets us free from the powerful pull of painful memories.

Important Steps for Sexual Victims

There are two Steps to Freedom in Christ which will be extremely critical for you if you have been victimized by rape, incest, or other forms of sexual abuse: forgiving those who have offended you and breaking bonds that were formed when you were violated sexually.

The area of forgiveness can be most difficult for anyone who has suffered severely at the hands of a sexual offender. If you fall into this category, you may be in special need of finding a trustworthy individual to help you through this process. To forgive those who offended you means to let go of that person's offense. As difficult as it may be, forgiving the offender actually sets you free from their offense. It is an act of your will, not your feelings. You must choose to forgive for your own sake. It is the only way to be free of the bitterness that may have filled your heart.

As you take this step, Satan may try to convince you that forgiving the offender somehow makes what he or she did right. That's a lie. What the offender did to you can never be justified. You were stripped of your safety and used for someone else's pleasure. That person owes you a debt that can never be paid. But that's between God and the offender. The wrongs of the past do not become right when you forgive, but by forgiving you can be free of them.

Another tactic Satan may employ to keep you from forgiving is to convince you that you will be relinquishing your only defense against future violations from the offender: your anger. But our emotions were not designed to be a defense. They are only an internal warning system about what is happening to us. Your anger is a signal that you have been threatened or hurt and that you need to take action. The proper action is to forgive and then to take appropriate steps so the offender cannot hurt you again. When you deal with the offense, the anger will dissipate.

Satan may also insist that you have a right to revenge for what the offender did to you. But only God can deal with that person justly. You must leave vengeance to God.

Others protest, "Why should I forgive? You don't know how badly that person hurt me." But they are still hurting you! How do you stop the pain? The only way is to break the bondage and forgive from your heart. When you choose to forgive by facing all the painful memories connected with your abuse—the hate, the hurt, the absolute ugliness of what the offender did to you—you can and will be free. Step 3 in Appendix A will guide you through this important process.

Another vital step to gaining freedom from past offenses is to ask God to break the spiritual bonds that were formed when you were violated sexually. When a husband and wife consummate their marriage physically, they become one. A physical, emotional, and spiritual bond is formed. When your body was used for unrighteous sexual purposes, a bond was formed—not the holy bond God ordained for marriage, but an unholy bond. You may have been an unwitting or unwilling participant in this union, but a bond was formed nevertheless.

I have learned through much experience to encourage everyone who comes to us for help to ask the Lord to reveal every sexual use of their body as an instrument of unrighteousness. Many people will openly share one or two experiences, but when they sincerely pray this prayer, I hear all the other sexual experiences they had forgotten or didn't want to mention. Once the experiences are brought to light and renounced the bonds can be broken. Step 6 in Appendix A will guide you through the process of breaking spiritual bonds which have been formed in the past.

Beth is a classic example of the bondage that results from sexual promiscuity and abuse. She was a Christian girl who had so many problems that her parents made an appointment for her to see me. Her behavior was tearing up her parents and destroying their Christian home. Usually nothing good comes from appointments made by parents for children who don't want to be helped. But Beth's parents assured me that the girl wanted to see me.

Beth's opening statement was, "I don't want to get right with God or anything like that." Hiding my own frustration, I said, "I can accept that. But since you're here, maybe we could try to resolve some of the conflicts in your life." Beth thought that would be okay. She told me the story of being date-raped by the campus hero at her high school. At the time she was too embarrassed to tell anyone about it, and she had no idea how to resolve it. Having lost her virginity, she became sexually promiscuous, living off and on with a real loser.

I asked Beth's permission to lead her through the Steps to Freedom in Christ, and she agreed. When I invited her to ask the Lord to reveal to her mind every sexual use of her body as an instrument of unrighteousness, she said, "That would be embarrassing." So I stepped out of the room while my female partner helped her through the process. That night she was singing in church for the first time in years. She was free.

After years of helping people find their freedom in Christ we have observed several generalities. First, if people have had "unholy" sex, they don't seem to enjoy "holy" sex. I have counseled many wives who can't stand to be touched by their husbands. In hard cases they are actually repulsed by the idea until they break the bondages that come from sex outside the will of God. Incredibly, their feelings toward their spouse change almost immediately after finding their freedom in Christ.

We have also noticed that promiscuity before marriage seems to lead to a lack of fulfillment after marriage. The fun and excitement of sex outside the will of God leaves one in bondage. If it was consensual, the bondages only increase as they attempt to satisfy their lust. If it wasn't consensual (they were forced to submit), they shut down and remain in bondage to their past until it is resolved. They lack the freedom to enter into a loving relationship where there is mutual expression of love and trust. We have them renounce those previous sexual uses of their body, commit their bodies to God as a living sacrifice, and reserve the sexual use of their bodies for their spouses only.

In the cases of rape and incest, someone has used their bodies as instruments of unrighteousness. Tragically, they have become one flesh. I want to scream "not fair" when some sick person defiles another person's "temple" against the will of that person who is trying to use it to glorify God. It's not fair! It's sick, but we live in a sick world. It is no different than Antiochus defiling the Temple against the will of those who died trying to save it. The good news is we can be free from such violations. We can renounce those uses of our body, submit to God, and resist the devil (James 4:7). We can and must forgive those who have abused us.

Ideally, you should read my books *Victory over the Darkness* and *The Bondage Breaker* before going through the Steps to Freedom in Christ. You need to know who you are as a child of God and how to walk by faith. You must understand how to renew your mind and realize the spiritual nature of the battle that is taking place there. You must understand the spiritual authority and protection every believer possesses in Christ.

The Steps to Freedom in Christ are not an end in themselves. They really offer a new beginning. For some people, the first time through the steps will represent the first major victory in a war that continues on. The following testimony from a man who was formerly trapped in nearly every form of sexual bondage mentioned in this book, illustrates the process of securing freedom in Christ one victory at a time.

My dad left our home when I was four years old. Every day I cried out to God to bring my daddy home. But he never came back. So my mother, my brother, and I moved in with my grandparents. I disconnected from God early in life because no one tried to explain why He never answered my pleas.

One night my grandfather undressed in front of me and my grandmother. He had an erection. Although he wouldn't have done anything to hurt me, my grandfather's act of indiscretion left a terrible mark in my mind which surfaced years later.

I thought my grandfather loved me. It didn't matter to me that he had been unfaithful to my grandmother, that he had sexually abused my mother, and that he was becoming an alcoholic. In the absence of my father, as a young boy I bonded with my grandfather. When my mother remarried and we moved away, I felt like I lost my father for a second time. But I didn't bother to ask God for help because I felt He had let me down.

We moved every year as I grew up. Every time I made a friend, we moved again, keeping the wounds of abandonment and loneliness painful. I grieved over every loss and did everything to protect myself from being hurt again.

I believed that I was different from most boys. I started playing sexually with some of my male friends during grade school. Voices in my head told me it was okay because I was born that way. I had a terrible male void in my life and my heart burned with desire. The memory of seeing my grandfather with an erection prompted a fascination with seeing boys and men naked. Voyeurism became a way of life for me.

Meanwhile, my own family was being ripped apart by conflict. The squabbles and fights mortified me. I was a loyal and sensitive kid who carried a deep concern for everyone in my family. I tried to convince my friends' parents to adopt me in order to escape the turmoil, but it didn't work. I finally detached completely from my mother and brother.

As an adolescent and young adult, I threw myself into the gay world. I was addicted watching men in public rest rooms and visited gay bars almost every night. When I found a gay lover, I thought I had finally met a man who would love me and stay with me forever. I was emotionally co-dependent on him. When the relationship ended after three years, I fell into a deep depression. I was emotionally bankrupt and lost. News of my brother's death added to my sense of despair and abandonment.

At his funeral I purchased a Bible, but I didn't know why. I kept it on my nightstand with a cross someone gave me. I didn't dare move them. I was terrified at night. I felt a horrifying dark presence around me at night. Someone told me to hold the cross and yell, "I bind you in the name of Jesus Christ of Nazareth!" I did so night after night with the covers pulled up to my neck. But something kept tormenting me night after night.

I finally started reading the Bible and attending church. I accepted the Lord at a baptism service and left the gay lifestyle completely. I studied the Word seriously, but with my background it was easy to fall into legalism. I didn't understand grace and forgiveness. The Bible talked a lot about sexual immorality and clearly forbade homosexual behavior. I asked myself, "If I am a Christian, why do I still feel the same homosexual tendencies?" The more I tried to do what the Bible said and what others expected of me, the more guilty I felt. I didn't dare tell anyone what I was feeling. The voyeurism became intense and triggered an uncontrollable bondage to masturbation.

As I began teaching a Sunday School class, the voices in my head condemned me daily and accused me of being a hypocrite. I believed them. I was tormented. The more I fought back by reading my Bible and serving the Lord, the greater the oppression became. My mind was ruled by immoral thoughts. I experienced intense sexual dreams. I was out of control and backsliding quickly. I found myself back in public rest rooms. I talked to Christian counselors and pastors, but no one seemed to offer a workable solution to my problem. I wanted so badly to know and serve the Lord.

A friend who was aware of my struggle gave me a copy of *Victory over the Darkness* by Neil Anderson. As I began reading it, the book seemed to be written about me. For the first time I understood how I got into my horrible condition and how I could get out of it. No one had ever told me that I was a child of God, that God had chosen me as His friend, and that He loved me specifically. I had learned about God intellectually, but through reading this book I finally met my gentle and loving heavenly Father personally.

When I read *The Bondage Breaker*, I knew I was spiritually oppressed. I had been involved in almost everything in the non-Christian spiritual experience inventory at the end of the book. I began to understand my oppressive thought life, rampant voyeurism, and low sense of worth. I discovered that realizing I am a child of God was the answer to breaking the destructive cycle that had been present in my family for generations.

I learned that Jesus is the bondage breaker and that I have authority over the kingdom of darkness because I am seated with Christ in the heavenlies. However, the more I embraced these truths, the more I was attacked. I was falling apart emotionally. I had to see Neil Anderson.

I attended one of his conferences and my entire life was changed. One of his staff met with me in a four-hour session. No one has ever wanted to spend that much time with me. I felt free for the first time in my life. Still, my desperate need for affirmation prevented me from being totally honest in the counseling session.

Two days later Neil talked about forgiving others. I asked him if a person has to cry when they forgive someone. He didn't answer. He made me think about it. On the way back to the motel, I told the Lord that I really wanted to forgive my dad and step-dad for not validating me. Then the Lord let me feel the pain of not being validated. He gave me a glimpse of His pain on the cross. I cried so hard I could hardly drive. Then I thought of the women in my life that had hurt me so badly. The flood gates opened as I forgave each person from my heart.

I was free, but Neil shared with me that people who have been in bondage a long time are more like onions than bananas. You peel a banana once, and that's it. But an onion has many layers. He cautioned me that I had successfully worked through at least one layer of my problem. Other layers may surface, but at least I knew how to respond when they did.

After a couple of months, the glow of my freedom subsided. I started to backslide and return to voyeurism. I read Neil's books, *Released from Bondage* and *Walking in the Light*. I fought back against the attack and worked through the issues. Another layer of the onion was peeled away. I felt renewed again, but also worn out from the battle. I wasn't reading the Word or praying much. I didn't feel like doing it.

So I started reading Neil and Joanne's devotional, *Daily in Christ*. I was filled with guilt because of my mental lapses into voyeurism and masturbation. How could I teach Sunday School and be such a hypocrite? I told the Lord that I really loved Him and wanted to serve Him. Then I decided to prove it. I was always fearful of vows, but I made one. I told the Lord that I was His child and that I was going to be baptized again. I knew I didn't have to and that baptism didn't save me, but I wanted to erect a milestone for the Lord like the Israelites did when they crossed the Jordan.

I made the vow and the Lord honored it beyond my wildest anticipation. He confirmed in me that I was a child of God and that He loved me. Once I submitted myself completely to Him and stopped trying to fix myself, He could do it for me.

The masturbation stopped instantaneously and has never come back. The voyeurism has also stopped. I have learned what it means to take every thought captive in obedience to Christ. Now I measure everything that comes into my mind against what the Lord says in His Word, and the truth has set me free.

Now that I know I am a child of God, there is no more low self-worth, inferiority, obsessive, negative, or perverse thoughts, or secret behavior. I busted through that last layer of the onion like a rocket. There may be more layers ahead, but this time I am armed with the Lord's belt of truth.

Staying Free

Your experience of going through the Steps to Freedom in Christ and being set free from bondages may be different from anyone else's. Why? Because each individual is unique, and each has his or her own unique set of conflicts to resolve. Some people are elated at the overwhelming sense of peace they feel for the very first time. Others may have to work through many layers yet to come. God graciously doesn't hurry us through everything at once, especially if the process is difficult. Getting free and staying free in Christ are two different issues.

Paul wrote, "It was for freedom that Christ set us free" (Galatians 5:1). Once we have tasted freedom in Christ, how do we keep it? It is nurtured and maintained by continuing to stand in the truth of who we are in Christ. Paul completes the verse by encouraging, "Stand firm, then, and do not let yourselves be burdened again by the yoke of slavery." Freedom is our inheritance, but we must not turn our freedom in Christ into ritualistic rules and regulations—legalism—or an opportunity to indulge our fleshly nature—license (Galatians 5:13). The steps you take to find your freedom are not the end of a journey but the beginning of a walk in the Spirit. Paul instructed, "Live by the Spirit, and you will not gratify the desires of the old nature" (Galatians 5:16).

Important Relationships

Staying free also involves being in positive relationships with others. We absolutely need God, but we also desperately need the loving fellowship of the body of Christ. There are different kinds of relationships, and we need each of them. If you are married, God will use your spouse, even if he or she is not a believer, to help conform your life to His image. No other human knows you better than the members of your family. Giving your marriage partner access to your heart through honest communication makes your relationship vulnerable to change and intensifies healthy intimacy. In our homes and churches, we must speak the truth in love (Ephesians 4:25) and walk in the light (1 John 1:6-8). There is always the possibility of discord in any human relationship, but if interaction is founded on seeking the truth, conflicts will be minimized and resolvable. The fewer the restrictions there are to intimacy in your marriage, the closer you will come to marital harmony at every dimension—physically, emotionally, and spiritually.

Another important relationship for you to cultivate is with a spiritually mature believer of your gender—a big brother or big sister in the faith. Ask this person to disciple you and spur you on in your Christian life. A mature Christian will be your spiritual reference point to help you maintain your walk before the Lord, providing accountability and modeling for your walk of faith. Ask God to direct you to the individual whom He has chosen to fill this role at this time in your life.

You also need to be involved in a group of Christian peers who have taken the Steps to Freedom in Christ and understand your journey. You may be able to meet this need by joining a small Bible study group at your church where others can come alongside you to provide objectivity, to encourage you to grow, and to keep you on track. You will discover with others that maturity is not instantaneous but gradual. Together you will help pace each other and stimulate forward motion in your daily walk.

Consider also getting involved in a Bible-based support group with others who have struggled with sexual bondage, people who understand exactly what you have been through and what you face every day. There are a variety of support groups in nearly every community, and many large churches sponsor such groups. Seek out a group whose central focus is Jesus Christ.

Support groups can provide a positive, supportive atmosphere as you mature emotionally, physically, socially, and spiritually. Relationships formed and nurtured in the safety of a support group can be a springboard into other positive relationships.

Beware of the attitude, fostered by some support groups, that you will be in recovery from spiritual bondage for life. Recovery may take time and effort. But inferring that the process has no end can seriously hamper the process of maturity. My colleague, Russ, talked to someone recently who illustrates this problem.

Years ago, Byron attended a support group Russ co-led. Byron came to the group for help in overcoming dependency on certain addictive behaviors. At the same time he continued to attend two other recovery groups. As Russ talked to Byron during a meeting, it was clear that he had achieved only minimal progress over the years in mastering his negative thoughts and behaviors. Jesus had indeed become a significant part of Byron's recovery experience, but he continued to struggle with the same destructive behaviors. In tearful voice he told Russ, "I don't feel like I'm making any headway. I'm frustrated that the process is taking so long, even though I know I will always be in a process of recovery from my addictions." Byron appeared to be stuck in the recovery process with no hope of moving on to further personal growth and spiritual maturity. Some support groups seem to validate the slow and tedious process that they believe necessary to eventually overcome addictive behaviors.

This is certainly not everyone's experience with support or recovery groups. Many people have taken advantage of biblically based support groups and have reoriented their lives to the truth of God's Word, and I certainly encourage that.

Freedom in Christ from sexual bondage and other captivating behaviors is a gift that God offers to all His children. This gift is available in abundance and is completely satisfying. It is my prayer that, as you walk through the Steps to Freedom in Christ in Appendix A, you will revel in the truth of God's forgiveness and His freeing grace. He alone is the way of escape.

Appendix

Steps to Freedom in Christ

I f you have received Christ as your personal Savior, He has set you free through His victory over sin and death on the cross. If you are not experiencing freedom, it may be because you have not stood firm in the faith or actively taken your place in Christ. It is the Christian's responsibility to do whatever is necessary to maintain a right relationship with God. Your eternal destiny is not at stake; you are already secure in Christ. But your daily victory is at stake if you fail to claim and maintain your position in Christ.

You are not the helpless victim caught between two nearly equal but opposite heavenly superpowers; Satan is a deceiver. Only God is omnipotent (all-powerful), omnipresent (always-present), and omniscient (all-knowing). Sometimes the reality of sin and the presence of evil may seem more real than the presence of God, but that is part of Satan's deception. Satan is a defeated foe, and we are in Christ. A true knowledge of God and our identity in Christ are the greatest determinants of our mental health. A false concept of God, a distorted understanding of who we are as children of God, and the misplaced deification of Satan (attributing God's attributes to Satan) are the greatest contributors to mental illness.

As you prepare to go through the Steps to Freedom in Christ, you need to remember that the only power Satan has is the power of the lie. As soon as you expose the lie, Satan's power is broken. The battle is for your mind. If Satan can get you to believe a lie, he can control your life. But you don't have to let him control you. If you are going through the steps by yourself, don't pay attention to any lying, intimidating thoughts in your mind, such as, "This isn't going to work," "God doesn't love me," "I'm just going to fall back into the same traps of sexual sin," etc. Such thoughts are lies from the pit. They can only control you if you believe them, so don't.

If you are going through the steps with a pastor, counselor, or prayer partner (which we strongly recommend if there has been severe trauma in your life), share any thoughts you have which are in opposition to what you are attempting to do. As soon as you expose the lie, the power of Satan is broken. You must cooperate with the person trying to help you by sharing what is going on inside.

Knowing the nature of the battle for our minds, we can pray authoritatively to stop any interference. The steps begin with a suggested prayer and declaration. If you are going through the steps by yourself, you will need to change some of the personal pronouns; ("I" instead of "we," etc.).

Prayer

Dear heavenly Father, we acknowledge Your presence in this room and in our lives. You are the only omniscient (all-knowing), omnipotent (all-powerful),

and omnipresent (always-present) God. We are dependent upon You, for apart from Christ we can do nothing. We stand in the truth that all authority in heaven and on earth has been given to the resurrected Christ, and because we are in Christ, we share that authority in order to make disciples and set captives free. We ask You to fill us with Your Holy Spirit and lead us into all truth. We pray for Your complete protection and ask for Your guidance. In Jesus' name we pray. Amen.

Declaration

In the name and authority of the Lord Jesus Christ, we command Satan and all evil spirits to release (name) in order that (name) can be free to know and choose to do the will of God. As children of God seated with Christ in the heavenlies, we agree that every enemy of the Lord Jesus Christ is bound and gagged to silence. We say to Satan and all his evil workers that he cannot inflict any pain or in any way prevent God's will from being accomplished in (name).

The following seven specific steps will help you experience the full freedom and victory that Christ purchased for you on the cross. These steps will help you walk free of many areas of bondage, but in this book specific application is made to areas of sexual bondage. Realizing your freedom will be the result of what you choose to believe, confess, forgive, renounce, and forsake. No one can do it for you. The battle for your mind can only be won as you personally choose truth.

As you go through these Steps to Freedom, remember that Satan will be defeated only if you confront him verbally. He cannot read your mind, and he is under no obligation to obey your thoughts. Only God has complete knowledge of your mind. As you take each step, it is important that you submit to God inwardly and resist the devil by reading aloud each prayer, verbally renouncing Satan, confessing sin, forgiving offenders, etc.

You will be taking a fierce moral inventory and making a rock-solid commitment to truth. If your problems stem from a source other than those covered in these steps, you have nothing to lose by going through them. If you are sincere, the only thing that can happen is that you will get right with God on these issues.

STEP 1: COUNTERFEIT VERSUS REAL

Many roots of sexual perversion and bondage are found in false teaching and the occult. So the first step to freedom in Christ is to renounce your previous or current involvements with satanically inspired occult practices and false religions. You need to renounce any activity and group which denies Jesus Christ, offers guidance through any source other than the absolute authority of the written Word of God, or requires secret initiations, ceremonies, or covenants.

In order to help you assess your spiritual experiences, begin this step by asking God to reveal false guidance and counterfeit religious experiences.

> Dear heavenly Father, I ask You to guard my heart and my mind and reveal to me any and all involvement I have had either knowingly or unknowingly with cultic or occult practices, false religions, and false teachers. In Jesus' name I pray. Amen.

Using the "Non-Christian Spiritual Experience Inventory" shown below, circle any activities in which you have been involved in any way. This list is not exhaustive, but it will guide you in identifying non-Christian experiences. Add any other involvements you have had. Even if you "innocently" participated in something or watched someone do it, you should write it on your list to renounce, just in case you unknowingly gave Satan a foothold.

Non-Christian
Spiritual Experience Inventory

Astral projection
Automatic writing
Bahaism
Black and white magic
Black Muslim
Blood pacts or cut yourself in a
  destructive way
Christian Science
Clairvoyance
Dungeons and Dragons
Eckankar
Father Divine
Fetishism (worship of objects)
Fortune-telling
Ghosts
Hare Krishna
Herbert W. Armstrong
Hinduism
Incubi and succubi (sexual spirits)
Islam
Jehovah's Witnesses
Magic eight ball
Masons
Materialization
Mental suggestions or attempts to
  swap minds

Mormonism
New Age
Ouija board
Rod & pendulum (dowsing)
Rosicrucianism
Roy Masters
Science of Creative Intelligence
Science of the Mind
Seance
Self-hypnosis
Silva Mind Control
Speaking in trance
Spirit guides
Swedenborgianism
Table-lifting
Tarot cards
Telepathy
Theosophical Society
Transcendental Meditation
Unification Church
Unitarianism
The Way International
Yoga
Zen Buddhism
Other

1. Have you ever been hypnotized, attended a New Age or parapsychology seminar, or consulted a medium, spiritist, or channeler? Explain.

2. Do you now have or have you ever had an imaginary friend or spirit guide offering you guidance or companionship? Explain.

3. Have you ever heard voices in your mind or had repeating and nagging thoughts condemning you or that were foreign to what you believe or feel, like there was a dialogue going on in your head? Explain.

4. What other spiritual experiences have you had that would be considered out of the ordinary?

5. Have you ever been involved in satanic ritual of any form? Explain.

When you are confident that your list is complete, confess and renounce each involvement, whether active or passive, by praying aloud the following prayer, repeating it separately for each item on your list:

Lord, I confess that I have participated in (activity). I ask your forgiveness, and I renounce (activity).

If you have had any involvement in satanic ritual or heavy occult activity (or you suspect past involvement because of blocked memories, severe nightmares, or sexual dysfunction or bondage), you need to state aloud the special renunciations which follow. Read across the page, renouncing first the item in the column for the Kingdom of Darkness and then affirming its counterpart in the Kingdom of Light. Continue down the page in this manner.

Renounce all satanic rituals, covenants, and assignments as the Lord allows you to remember them. Some people who have been subjected to satanic ritual abuse have developed multiple personalities in order to survive. Nevertheless, continue through the Steps to Freedom in order to resolve all you can remember. It is important that you resolve the demonic strongholds first. Eventually every personality must be accessed, and each one must resolve his or her issues and agree to come together in Christ. You may need someone who understands spiritual conflict to help you with this.

Special Renunciations
for Satanic Ritual Involvement

Kingdom of Darkness	Kingdom of Light
I renounce ever signing my name over to Satan	I announce that my name is now written in the Lamb's Book of Life.
I renounce any ceremony where I may have been wed to Satan.	I announce that I am the bride of Christ.
I renounce any and all covenants that I made with Satan.	I announce that I am a partaker of the New Covenant with Christ.
I renounce all satanic assignments for my life, including duties, marriage, and children.	I announce and commit myself to know and do only the will of God and accept only His guidance.

I renounce all spirit guides assigned to me.

I announce and accept only the leading of the Holy Spirit.

I renounce ever giving of my blood in the service of Satan.

I trust only in the shed blood of my Lord Jesus Christ.

I renounce ever eating of flesh or drinking of blood for satanic worship.

By faith I eat only the symbolic flesh and drink only the symbolic blood of Jesus in Holy Communion.

I renounce any and all guardians and Satanist parents that were assigned to me.

I announce that God is my Father and the Holy Spirit is my Guardian by whom I am sealed.

I renounce any baptism in blood or urine whereby I am identified with Satan.

I announce that I have been baptized into Christ Jesus and my identity is now in Christ.

I renounce any and all sacrifices that were made on my behalf by which Satan may claim ownership of me.

I announce that only the sacrifice of Christ has any hold on me. I belong to Him. I have been purchased by the blood of the Lamb.

STEP 2: DECEPTION VERSUS TRUTH

Truth is the revelation of God's Word, but we need to acknowledge the truth in the inner self (Psalm 51:6). When David lived a lie after committing adultery and murder, he suffered greatly. When he finally found freedom by acknowledging the truth, he wrote, "How blessed is the man . . . in whose spirit is no deceit" (Psalm 32:2). We are to lay aside falsehood and speak the truth in love (Ephesians 4:15,25). A mentally healthy person is one who is in touch with reality and relatively free of anxiety. Both qualities should characterize the Christian who renounces deception and embraces the truth.

You doubtless became trapped in sexual bondage because you believed Satan's lies about sex and/or your sexuality. Begin this critical step by expressing aloud the following prayer regarding deceit and truth. Don't let the enemy accuse you with thoughts such as "I wish I could believe this, but I can't" or any other lies in opposition to what you are proclaiming. Even if you have difficulty doing so, you need to pray the prayer and read the doctrinal affirmation which follows.

> Dear heavenly Father, I know that You desire truth in the inner self and that facing this truth is the way of liberation (John 8:32). I acknowledge that I have been deceived by the father of lies (John 8:44) and that I have deceived myself (1 John 1:8). I pray in the name of the Lord Jesus Christ that You, heavenly Father, will rebuke all deceiving spirits by virtue of the shed blood and resurrection of the Lord Jesus Christ. By faith I have received You into my life and I am now seated with Christ in the heavenlies (Ephesians 2:6). I acknowledge that I

have the responsibility and authority to resist the devil, and when I do so, he will flee from me. I now ask the Holy Spirit to guide me into all truth (John 6:13). I ask You to "search me, O God, and know my heart; try me and know my anxious thoughts; and see if there be any hurtful way in me, and lead me in the everlasting way" (Psalm 139:23,24 NASB). In Jesus' name I pray. Amen.

You may want to pause at this point to consider some of Satan's deceptive schemes. In addition to false teachers, false prophets, and deceiving spirits, you can deceive yourself. Now that you are alive in Christ and forgiven, you never have to live a lie or defend yourself. Christ is your defense. How have you deceived or attempted to defend yourself according to the following?

Self-deception

_____ Being a hearer and not a doer of the Word (James 1:22; 4:17).

_____ Saying you have no sin (1 John 1:8).

_____ Thinking you are something when you are not (Galatians 6:3).

_____ Thinking you are wise in this age (1 Corinthians 3:18,19).

_____ Thinking you will not reap what you sow (Galatians 6:7).

_____ Thinking the unrighteous will inherit the kingdom of God (1 Corinthians 6:9).

_____ Thinking you can associate with bad company and not be corrupted (1 Corinthians 15:33).

Self-defense (defending ourselves instead of trusting in Christ)

_____ Denial (conscious or subconscious).

_____ Fantasy (escape from the real world).

_____ Emotional insulation (withdrawal to avoid rejection).

_____ Regression (reverting back to a less threatening time).

_____ Displacement (taking out frustrations on others).

_____ Projection (blaming others).

_____ Rationalization (defending self through verbal excursion).

For the self-deceiving attitudes and actions which have been true of you, pray aloud:

Lord, I agree that I have been deceived in the area of (attitude or action). Thank You for forgiving me. I commit myself to know and follow Your truth. Amen.

Choosing the truth may be difficult if you have been deceived and living a lie for many years. You may need to seek professional help to weed out the defense mechanisms you have depended upon to survive. Knowing that you are forgiven and accepted as God's child is what sets you free to face reality and declare your dependence on Him.

Faith is the biblical response to the truth, and believing the truth is a choice. When someone says, "I want to believe God, but I just can't," he is being deceived. Of course you can believe God! Faith is something you *decide to do,* not something you *feel like doing.* Believing the truth doesn't make it true. It's true; therefore we believe it. The New Age movement is distorting the truth by saying we create reality through what we believe. We can't create reality with our minds; we face reality. It's what or who you believe in that counts. Everybody believes in something, and everybody walks by faith according to what he or she believes. But if what you believe isn't true, then how you live won't be right.

Historically, the church has found great value in publicly declaring its beliefs. The Apostles' Creed and the Nicene Creed have been recited for centuries. Read aloud the following affirmation of faith, and do so again as often as necessary to renew your mind. Read it daily for several weeks.

Doctrinal Affirmation

I recognize that there is only one true and living God (Exodus 20:2,3) who exists as the Father, Son, and Holy Spirit, and that He is worthy of all honor, praise, and glory as the Creator, Sustainer, and Beginning and End of all things (Revelation 4:11; 5:9,10; Isaiah 43:1,7,21).

I recognize Jesus Christ as the Messiah, the Word who became flesh and dwelt among us (John

1:1,14). I believe that He came to destroy the works of Satan (1 John 3:8), that He disarmed the rulers and authorities and made a public display of them, having triumphed over them (Colossians 2:15).

I believe that God has proven His love for me because when I was still a sinner, Christ died for me (Romans 5:8). I believe that He delivered me from the domain of darkness and transferred me to His kingdom, and in Him I have redemption, the forgiveness of sins (Colossians 1:13,14).

I believe that I am now a child of God (1 John 3:1-3) and that I am seated with Christ in the heavenlies (Ephesians 2:6). I believe that I was saved by the grace of God through faith, that it was a gift and not the result of any works on my part (Ephesians 2:8).

I choose to be strong in the Lord and in the strength of His might (Ephesians 6:10). I put no confidence in the flesh (Philippians 3:3), for the weapons of warfare are not of the flesh (2 Corinthians 10:4). I put on the whole armor of God (Ephesians 6:10-20), and I resolve to stand firm in my faith and resist the evil one.

I believe that apart from Christ I can do nothing (John 15:5), so I declare myself dependent on Him. I choose to abide in Christ in order to bear much fruit and glorify the Lord (John 15:8). I announce to Satan that Jesus is my Lord (1 Corinthians 12:3), and I reject any counterfeit gifts or works of Satan in my life.

I believe that the truth will set me free (John 8:32) and that walking in the light is the only path of fellowship (1 John 1:7). Therefore, I stand against Satan's deception by taking every thought captive in obedience to Christ (2 Corinthians 10:5).

I declare that the Bible is the only authoritative standard (2 Timothy 3:15,16). I choose to speak the truth in love (Ephesians 4:15).

I choose to present my body as an instrument of righteousness, a living and holy sacrifice, and I renew my mind by the living Word of God in order that I may prove that the will of God is good, acceptable, and perfect (Romans 6:13; 12:1,2).

I put off the old self with its evil practices and put on the new self (Colossians 3:9,10), and I declare myself to be a new creature in Christ (2 Corinthians 5:17).

I ask You heavenly Father to fill me with Your Holy Spirit (Ephesians 5:18), lead me into all truth (John 16:13), and empower my life that I may live above sin and not carry out the desires of the flesh (Galatians 5:16). I crucify the flesh (Galatians 5:24) and choose to walk by the Spirit.

I renounce all selfish goals and choose the ultimate goal of love (1 Timothy 1:5). I choose to obey the two greatest commandments: to love the Lord my God with all my heart, soul, and mind, and to love my neighbor as myself (Matthew 22:37-39).

I believe that Jesus has all authority in heaven and on earth (Matthew 28:18) and that He is the head over all rule and authority (Colossians 2:10). I believe that Satan and his demons are subject to me in Christ because I am a member of Christ's body (Ephesians 1:19-23). Therefore I obey the command to submit to God and to resist the devil (James 4:7), and I command Satan in the name of Christ to leave my presence.

STEP 3: BITTERNESS VERSUS FORGIVENESS

You may have been mildly encouraged or strongly influenced into sexual sin and bondage by other persons. Perhaps a relative or neighbor sexually abused you as a child, or a sibling or schoolmate introduced you to pornography, or a boyfriend or girlfriend used you for sexual experimentation. You may harbor strong feelings against these people for their thoughtless, selfish, and sinful deeds—anger, hatred, bitterness, resentment.

You need to forgive others so that Satan cannot take advantage of you (2 Corinthians 2:10,11). As Christians, we are to be merciful just as our heavenly Father is merciful (Luke 6:36). We are to forgive as we have been forgiven (Ephesians 4:31,32). Use the following prayer to ask God to bring to your mind the names of people you need to forgive:

> Dear heavenly Father, I thank You for the riches of Your kindness, forbearance, and patience, knowing that Your kindness has led me to repentance (Romans 2:4). I confess that I have not extended that same patience and kindness toward others who have offended me, but instead I have harbored bitterness and resentment. I pray that during this time of self-examination You will bring to my mind the people I have not forgiven in order that I may do so (Matthew 18:35). I ask this in the precious name of Jesus. Amen.

As names come to mind, make a list of only the names. Include at the end of your list "myself." Forgiving yourself is accepting God's cleansing and forgiveness.

Also, write "thoughts against God." Thoughts raised up against the knowledge of God will usually result in angry feelings toward Him. Technically, we don't forgive God because He cannot commit any sin. But you need to specifically renounce false expectations and thoughts about God and agree to release any anger you have toward Him.

Before you pray to forgive the people on your list, stop and consider what forgiveness is, what it is not, what decision you will be making, and what the consequences will be.

Forgiveness is not forgetting. People who try to forget find that they cannot. God says He will remember our sins no more (Hebrews 10:17), but God, being omniscient, cannot forget. "Remember our sins no more" means that God will never use the past against us (Psalm 103:12). Forgetting may be the result of forgiveness, but it is never the means of forgiveness. When we bring up the past against others, we are saying we haven't forgiven them.

Forgiveness is a choice, a crisis of the will. Since God requires us to forgive, it is something we can do. But forgiveness is difficult for us because it pulls against our concept of justice. We want revenge for offenses suffered. However, we are told never to take our own revenge (Romans 12:19). You say, "Why should I let these people off the hook?" That is precisely the problem. You are still hooked to them, still bound by your past. You will let them off your hook, but they are never off God's hook. He will deal with them fairly, something we cannot do.

You say, "You don't understand how much these people hurt me!" By not forgiving them, you are still being hurt by them. How do you stop the pain? Forgive. You don't forgive others for their sake; you do it for your sake, so you can be free. Your need to forgive isn't an issue between you and the offender; it's between you and God.

Forgiveness is agreeing to live with the consequences of another person's sin. Forgiveness is costly. You pay the price of the evil you forgive. You're going to live with those consequences whether you want to or not; your only choice is whether you will do so in the bitterness of unforgiveness or the freedom of forgiveness. Jesus took the consequences of your sin upon Himself. All true forgiveness is substitutionary, because no one really forgives without bearing the consequences of the other person's sin. God the Father "made Him who had no sin to be sin for us, so that in him we might become the righteousness of God" (2 Corinthians 5:21).

Where is the justice? It is the cross of Christ that makes forgiveness legally and morally right: "The death he died, he died to sin once for all" (Romans 6:10).

How do you forgive from your heart? You acknowledge the hurt and the hate. If your forgiveness doesn't visit the emotional core of your life, it will be incomplete. Many people feel the pain of interpersonal offenses, but they won't or don't know how to acknowledge it. Let God bring the pain to the surface so He can deal with it. This is where the healing takes place.

Decide that you will bear the burdens of their offenses by not using the past against them in the future. This doesn't mean you must tolerate sin; you must always take a stand against sin.

Don't wait to forgive until you feel like forgiving; you will never get there. Feelings take time to heal after the choice to forgive is made and Satan has lost his place

(Ephesians 4:26,27). Freedom is what will be gained, not a feeling.

As you pray, God may bring to mind offending people and experiences you have totally forgotten. Let Him do it even if it is painful. Remember, you are doing this for your sake. God wants you to be free. Don't rationalize or explain the offender's behavior. Forgiveness is dealing with your pain and leaving the other person to God. Positive feelings will follow in time; freeing yourself from the past is the critical issue right now.

Don't say, "Lord, please help me to forgive," because He is already helping you. Don't say, "Lord, I want to forgive," because you are bypassing the hard-core choice to forgive, which is your responsibility. Stay with each individual until you are sure you have dealt with all the remembered pain— what the offender did, how he or she hurt you, how he or she made you feel (rejected, unloved, unworthy, dirty, etc.).

You are now ready to forgive the people on your list so that you can be free in Christ, with those people no longer having any control over you. For each person on your list, pray aloud:

> Lord, I forgive (name) for (specifically identify all offenses and painful memories or feelings).

STEP 4: REBELLION VERSUS SUBMISSION

We live in a rebellious generation. Many people believe it is their right to sit in judgment of those in authority over them. But rebelling against God and His authority gives Satan an opportunity to attack. As our general, the Lord commands us to get into ranks and follow Him. He will not lead us into temptation, but He will deliver us from evil (Matthew 6:13).

You may have a problem with authority figures because someone you looked up to or followed was instrumental in your moral downfall. Perhaps a teacher or coach abused you. Perhaps an employer or spiritual leader took advantage of you sexually. You may not trust or want to submit to other leaders because of what happened to you.

We have two biblical responsibilities in regard to authority figures: Pray for them and submit to them. The only time God permits us to disobey earthly leaders is when they require us to do something morally wrong before God or attempt to rule outside the realm of their authority.

Pray the following prayer:

> Dear heavenly Father, You have said that rebellion is as the sin of witchcraft and insubordination is as iniquity and idolatry (1 Samuel 15:23). I know that in action and attitude I have sinned against You with a rebellious heart. I ask Your forgiveness for my rebellion and pray that by the shed blood of the Lord Jesus Christ all ground gained by evil spirits because of my rebelliousness will be canceled. I pray that You will shed light on all my ways that I may know the full extent of my rebelliousness. I now choose to adopt a submissive spirit and a servant's heart. In the name of Christ Jesus, my Lord, I pray. Amen.

Being under authority is an act of faith. You are trusting God to work through His established lines of authority. There are times when employers, parents, and husbands violate the laws of civil government which are ordained by God to protect innocent people against abuse. In those cases you need to appeal to the state for your protection. In many states, the law requires such abuse to be reported.

In difficult cases, such as continuing abuse at home, you may need further counsel. In some cases, when earthly authorities have abused their position and require disobedience to God or a compromise in your commitment to Him, you need to obey God rather than man.

We are all admonished to submit to one another as equals in Christ (Ephesians 5:21). However, there are specific lines of authority in Scripture for the purpose of accomplishing common goals:

> Civil government (Romans 13:1-7; 1 Timothy 2:1-4; 1 Peter 2:13-17)
>
> Parents (Ephesians 6:1-3)
>
> Husband (1 Peter 3:1-4)
>
> Employer (1 Peter 2:18-23)
>
> Church leaders (Hebrews 13:17)
>
> God (Daniel 9:5,9)

Examine each area and ask God to forgive you for those times you have not been submissive:

> Lord, I agree I have been rebellious toward (name or position). Please forgive me for this rebellion. I choose to be submissive and obedient to Your Word. In Jesus' name I pray. Amen.

STEP 5: PRIDE VERSUS HUMILITY

Pride is a killer. Pride says, "I can do it! I can get myself out of this mess of immorality without God or anyone else's help." But we can't! We absolutely need God, and we desperately need each other. Paul wrote, "We . . . worship in the Spirit of God and glory in Christ Jesus and put no confidence in the flesh" (Philippians 3:3 NASB). Humility is confidence properly placed. We are to be "be strong in the Lord and in His mighty power" (Ephesians 6:10). James 4:6-10 and 1 Peter 5:1-10 reveal that spiritual conflict follows pride.

Use the following prayer to express your commitment to live humbly before God:

> Dear heavenly Father, You have said that pride goes before destruction and an arrogant spirit before stumbling (Proverbs 16:18). I confess that I have lived independently and have not denied myself, picked up my cross daily, and followed You (Matthew 16:24). In so doing, I have given ground to the enemy in my life. I have believed that I could be successful and live victoriously by my own strength and resources. I now confess that I have sinned against You by placing my will before Yours and by centering my life around self instead of You. I now renounce the self-life and by so doing cancel all the ground that has been gained in my members by the enemies of the Lord Jesus Christ. I pray that You will guide me so that I will do nothing from selfishness or empty conceit, but with humility of mind I will regard others as more important than myself (Philippians 2:3). Enable me through love to serve others and in honor prefer others (Romans

12:10). I ask this in the name of Christ Jesus my Lord. Amen.

Having made that commitment, now allow God to show you any specific areas of your life where you have been prideful, such as:

_____ Stronger desire to do my will than God's will

_____ More dependent upon my strengths and resources than God's

_____ Sometimes believe that my ideas and opinions are better than others'

_____ More concerned about controlling others than developing self-control

_____ Sometimes consider myself more important than others

_____ Tendency to think I have no needs

_____ Find it difficult to admit I was wrong

_____ Tendency to be more of a people-pleaser than a God-pleaser

_____ Overly concerned about getting the credit I deserve

_____ Driven to obtain the recognition that comes from degrees, titles, positions

_____ Often think I am more humble than others

_____ Other ways that you may have
thought more highly of yourself
than you should

For each of these that has been true in your life, pray
aloud:

Lord, I agree I have been prideful in the
area of _____. Please for-
give me for this pridefulness. I choose to
humble myself and place all my confidence
in You. Amen.

STEP 6: BONDAGE VERSUS FREEDOM

The next step to freedom deals with habitual sin.
People who have been caught in the trap of sin-confess-
sin-confess may need to follow the instructions of James
5:16: "Confess your sins to each other and pray for each
other so that you may be healed. The prayer of a righteous
man is powerful and effective." Seek out a righteous
person who will hold you up in prayer and to whom you
can be accountable. Others may need only the assurance
of 1 John 1:9: "If we confess our sins, he is faithful and
just and will forgive us our sins and purify us from all
unrighteousness." Confession is not saying "I'm sorry";
it's saying "I did it." Whether you need the help of others
or just the accountability of God, pray the following
prayer:

Dear heavenly Father, You have told us to
put on the Lord Jesus Christ and make no
provision for the flesh in regard to its lust

(Romans 13:14). I acknowledge that I have given in to fleshly lusts which wage war against my soul (1 Peter 2:11). I thank You that in Christ my sins are forgiven, but I have transgressed Your holy law and given the enemy an opportunity to wage war in my members (Romans 6:12,13; Ephesians 4:27; James 4:1; 1 Peter 5:8). I come before Your presence to acknowledge these sins and to seek Your cleansing (1 John 1:9) that I may be freed from the bondage of sin. I now ask You to reveal to my mind the ways that I have transgressed Your moral law and grieved the Holy Spirit. In Jesus' precious name I pray. Amen.

The deeds of the flesh are numerous. You may want to open your Bible to Galatians 5:19-21 and pray through the verses, asking the Lord to reveal the ways you have specifically sinned.

It is our responsibility not to allow sin to reign in our mortal bodies by not using our bodies as an instrument of unrighteousness (Romans 6:12,13). If you are struggling with habitual sexual sins (pornography, masturbation, sexual promiscuity) or experiencing sexual difficulty and lack of intimacy in your marriage, pray as follows:

Lord, I ask You to reveal to my mind every sexual use of my body as an instrument of unrighteousness. In Jesus' precious name I pray. Amen.

As the Lord brings to your mind every sexual use of your body, whether it was done to you (rape, incest, or any sexual molestation) or willingly by you, renounce every occasion:

> Lord, I renounce (name the specific use of your body) with (name the person) and ask You to break that bond.

Now commit your body to the Lord by praying:

> Lord, I renounce all these uses of my body as an instrument of unrighteousness and by so doing ask You to break all bondages Satan has brought into my life through that involvement. I confess my participation. I now present my body to You as a living sacrifice, holy and acceptable unto You, and I reserve the sexual use of my body only for marriage. I renounce the lie of Satan that my body is not clean, that it is dirty or in any way unacceptable as a result of my past sexual experiences. Lord, I thank You that You have totally cleansed and forgiven me, that You love and accept me unconditionally. Therefore, I can accept myself. And I choose to do so, to accept myself and my body as cleansed. In Jesus' name I pray. Amen.

Special Prayers for Specific Needs

Homosexuality

> Lord, I renounce the lie that You have created me or anyone else to be homosexual,

and I affirm that You clearly forbid homosexual behavior. I accept myself as a child of God and declare that You created me to be a (your sex). I renounce any bondages of Satan that have perverted my relationships with others. I announce that I am free to relate to the opposite sex in the way that You intended. In Jesus' name I pray. Amen.

Abortion

Lord, I confess that I did not assume stewardship of the life You entrusted to me, and I ask Your forgiveness. I choose to accept Your forgiveness by forgiving myself, and I now commit that child to You for Your care in eternity. In Jesus' name I pray. Amen.

Suicidal tendencies

I renounce the lie that I can find peace and freedom by taking my own life. Satan is a thief, and he comes to steal, kill, and destroy. I choose life in Christ, who said He came to give me life and to give it abundantly.

Eating disorders or cutting on yourself

I renounce the lie that my worthiness is dependent upon my appearance or performance. I renounce cutting myself, purging, or defecating as a means of cleansing myself of evil, and I announce that only the blood of the Lord Jesus Christ can cleanse me from my sin. I accept the reality that there may be sin present in me because of the lies I have believed and the wrongful use of my body, but I renounce the lie that I am evil or that any part of my body is evil. I announce the truth that I am totally accepted by Christ just as I am.

Substance abuse

Lord, I confess that I have misused substances (alcohol, tobacco, food, prescription or street drugs) for the purpose of pleasure, to escape reality, or to cope with difficult situations. the result has been the abuse of my body, the harmful programming of my mind, and the quenching of the Holy Spirit. I ask Your forgiveness, and I renounce any satanic connection or influence in my life through my misuse of chemicals or food. I cast my anxiety onto Christ, who loves me, and I commit myself to no longer yield to substance abuse but to the Holy Spirit. I ask You, heavenly Father, to fill me with Your Holy Spirit. In Jesus' name I pray. Amen.

After you have confessed all known sin, pray:

I now confess these sins to You and claim through the blood of the Lord Jesus Christ my forgiveness and cleansing. I cancel all ground that evil spirits have gained through my willful involvement in sin. I ask this in the wonderful name of my Lord and Savior Jesus Christ. Amen.

STEP 7: ACQUIESCENCE VERSUS RENUNCIATION

Acquiescence is passively agreeing with or giving in

to something or someone without conscious consent. For example, to some extent your sexual bondage may be the result of tendencies or curses passed on to you from your ancestors. You did not have a vote in the matter, and likely you have little or no knowledge of such activities. You only reaped the sad results.

The last step to freedom is to renounce the sins of your ancestors and any curses which may have been placed on you. In giving the Ten Commandments God said: "I, the Lord our God, am a jealous God, visiting the iniquity of the fathers on the children, on the third and fourth generations of those who hate Me" (Exodus 20:5 NASB).

Familiar spirits can be passed on from one generation to the next if they are not renounced and if your new spiritual heritage in Christ is not proclaimed. You are not guilty for the sin of any ancestor, but because of their sin, Satan may have gained access to your family. This is not to deny that many problems are transmitted genetically or acquired from an immoral atmosphere. All three conditions can predispose an individual to a particular sin. In addition, deceived people may try to curse you, or satanic groups may try to target you. You have all the authority and protection you need in Christ to stand against such curses and assignments.

In order to walk free from past influences, read the following declaration and prayer to yourself first so that you know exactly what you are declaring and asking. Then claim your position and protection in Christ by humbling yourself before God in prayer and making the declaration aloud.

Declaration

I here and now reject and disown all the sins of my ancestors. As one who has been delivered from the power of darkness and translated into the kingdom of God's dear Son, I cancel out all demonic working that has been passed on to me from my ancestors. As one who has been crucified and raised with Jesus Christ and who sits with Him in heavenly places, I renounce all satanic assignments that are directed toward me and my ministry, and I cancel every curse that Satan and his workers have put on me.

I announce to Satan and all his forces that Christ became a curse for me (Galatians 3:13) when He died for my sins on the cross. I reject any and every way in which Satan may claim ownership of me. I belong to the Lord Jesus Christ, who purchased me with His own blood. I reject all other blood sacrifices whereby Satan may claim ownership of me. I declare myself to be eternally and completely signed over and committed to the Lord Jesus Christ. By the authority that I have in Jesus Christ, I now command every familiar spirit and every enemy of the Lord Jesus Christ that is in or around me to leave my presence. I commit myself to my heavenly Father to do His will from this day forward.

Prayer

Dear heavenly Father, I come to You as Your child purchased by the blood of the Lord Jesus Christ. You are the Lord of the universe and the Lord of my life. I submit my body to You as an instrument of righteousness, a living sacrifice, that I may glorify You in my body. I now ask You to fill me with Your Holy Spirit. I commit myself to the renewing of my mind in order to prove that Your will is good, perfect, and acceptable for me. All this I do in the name and authority of the Lord Jesus Christ. Amen.

Once you have secured your freedom by going through these seven steps, you may find demonic influences attempting reentry days or even months later. One person shared that she heard a spirit say to her mind "I'm back" two days after she had been set free. "No, you're not!" she proclaimed aloud. The attack ceased immediately.

One victory does not constitute winning the war. Freedom must be maintained. After completing these steps, one jubilant lady asked, "Will I always be like this?" I told her that she would stay free as long as she remained in right relationship with God. "Even if you slip and fall," I encouraged, "you know how to get right with God again."

One victim of incredible atrocities shared this illustration: "It's like being forced to play a game with an ugly stranger in my own home. I kept losing and wanted to quit, but the ugly stranger wouldn't let me. Finally I called the police (a higher authority), and they came and escorted the stranger out. He knocked on the door trying to regain entry, but this time I recognized his voice and didn't let him in."

What a beautiful illustration of gaining freedom in Christ! We call upon Jesus, the ultimate authority, and He escorts the enemy out of our lives. Know the truth, stand firm, and resist the evil one. Seek out good Christian fellowship, and commit yourself to regular times of Bible study and prayer. God loves you and will never leave or forsake you.

After Care

Freedom must be maintained. You have won a very important battle in an ongoing war. Freedom is yours as long as you keep choosing truth and standing firm in the strength of the Lord. If new memories should surface or if you become aware of lies that you have believed or other non-Christian experiences you have had, renounce them and choose the truth. Some people have found it helpful to go through the steps again. As you do, read the instructions carefully.

For your encouragement and further study, read *Victory Over the Darkness* (or the youth version, *Stomping Out the Darkness*), *The Bondage Breaker* (or *The Bondage Breaker: Youth Edition*), and *Released from Bondage*. If you are a parent, read *The Seduction of Our Children*. *Walking in the Light* (formerly *Walking through the Darkness*) was written to help people understand God's guidance and discern counterfeit guidance.

Also, to maintain your freedom, we suggest the following:

1. Seek legitimate Christian fellowship where you can walk in the light and speak the truth in love.

2. Study your Bible daily. Memorize key verses. You may want to express the Doctrinal Affirmation daily and look up the verses.

3. Take every thought captive to the obedience of Christ. Assume responsibility for your thought life, reject the lie, choose the truth, and stand firm in your position in Christ.

4. Don't drift away! It is very easy to get lazy in your thoughts and revert back to old habit patterns of thinking. Share your struggles openly with a

trusted friend. You need at least one friend who will stand with you.

5. Don't expect another person to fight your battle for you. Others can help but they can't think, pray, read the Bible, or choose the truth for you.

6. Continue to seek your identity and sense of worth in Christ. Read *Living Free in Christ* and the devotional *Daily in Christ*. Renew your mind with the truth that your acceptance, security, and significance is in Christ by saturating your mind with the statements at the end of this chapter. Read the entire list aloud morning and evening over the next several weeks.

7. Commit yourself to daily prayer. You can pray the following suggested prayers often and with confidence:

Daily Prayer

Dear heavenly Father, I honor You as my sovereign Lord. I acknowledge that You are always present with me. You are the only all powerful and only wise God. You are kind and loving in all Your ways. I love You and I thank You that I am united with Christ and spiritually alive in Him. I choose not to love the world, and I crucify the flesh and all its passions.

I thank You for the life that I now have in Christ, and I ask You to fill me with Your Holy Spirit that I may live my life free from sin. I declare my dependence upon You, and I take my stand against Satan and all his lying ways. I choose to believe the truth, and I refuse to be discouraged. You are the God of all hope, and I am confident that You will meet my needs as I seek to live according to Your

Word. I express with confidence that I can live a responsible life through Christ, who strengthens me.

I now take my stand against Satan and command him and all his evil spirits to depart from me. I put on the whole armor of God. I submit my body as a living sacrifice and renew my mind by the living Word of God in order that I may prove that the will of God is good, acceptable, and perfect. I ask these things in the precious name of my Lord and Savior Jesus Christ. Amen.

Bedtime Prayer

Thank You, Lord, that You have brought me into Your family and have blessed me with every spiritual blessing in the heavenly realms in Christ. Thank You for providing this time of renewal through sleep. I accept it as part of Your perfect plan for Your children, and I trust You to guard my mind and my body during my sleep. As I have meditated on You and Your truth during this day, I choose to let these thoughts continue in my mind while I am asleep. I commit myself to You for Your protection from every attempt of Satan or his emissaries to attack me during sleep. I commit myself to You as my rock, my fortress, and my resting place. I pray in the strong name of the Lord Jesus Christ. Amen.

Cleansing Home/Apartment

After removing all articles of false worship from home/apartment, pray aloud in every room if necessary.

Heavenly Father, we acknowledge that You are

Lord of heaven and earth. In Your sovereign power and love, You have given us all things richly to enjoy. Thank You for this place to live. We claim this home for our family as a place of spiritual safety and protection from all the attacks of the enemy. As children of God seated with Christ in the heavenly realm, we command every evil spirit that would claim ground in the structures and furnishings of this place based on the activities of previous occupants to leave and never to return. We renounce all curses and spells utilized against this place. We ask You, heavenly Father, to post guardian angels around this home (apartment, condominium, room, etc.) to guard it from attempts of the enemy to enter and disturb Your purposes for us. We thank You, Lord, for doing this, and pray in the name of the Lord Jesus Christ. Amen.

Living in a Non-Christian Environment

After removing all articles of false worship from your room, pray aloud in the space allotted to you.

Thank You, heavenly Father, for my place to live and to be renewed by sleep. I ask You to set aside my room (my portion of the room) as a place of spiritual safety for me. I renounce any allegiance given to false gods or spirits by other occupants, and I renounce any claim to this room (space) by Satan based on activities of past occupants or myself. On the basis of my position as a child of God and a joint-heir with Christ who has all authority in heaven and on earth, I command all evil spirits to leave this place and never to return. I ask

You, heavenly Father, to appoint guardian angels to protect me while I live here. I pray this in the name of the Lord Jesus Christ. Amen.

In Christ I Am Accepted

- I am God's child (John 1:12).

- I am Christ's friend (John 15:15).

- I have been justified (Romans 5:1).

- I am united with the Lord, and I am one spirit with Him (1 Corinthians 6:17).

- I have been bought with a price. I belong to God (1 Corinthians 6:19,20).

- I am a member of Christ's body (1 Corinthians 12:27).

- I am a saint (Ephesians 1:1).

- I have been adopted as God's child (Ephesians 1:5).

- I have direct access to God through the Holy Spirit (Ephesians 2:18).

- I have been redeemed and forgiven of all my sins (Colossians 1:14).

- I am complete in Christ (Colossians 2:10).

In Christ I Am Secure

- I am free forever from condemnation (Romans 8:1,2).

- I am assured that all things work together for good (Romans 8:28).

- I am free from any condemning charges against me (Romans 8:31-34).

- I cannot be separated from the love of God (Romans 8:35-39)

- I have been established, anointed, and sealed by God (2 Corinthians 1:21,22).
- I am hidden with Christ in God (Colossians 3:3).
- I am confident that the good work that God has begun in me will be perfected (Philippians 1:6).
- I am a citizen of heaven (Philippians 3:20).
- I have not been given a spirit of fear but of power, love, and a sound mind (2 Timothy 1:7).
- I can find grace and mercy in time of need (Hebrews 4:16).
- I am born of God, and the evil one cannot touch me (1 John 5:18).

In Christ I Am Significant

- I am the salt and light of the earth (Matthew 5:13,14).
- I am a branch of the true vine, a channel of His life (John 15:1,5).
- I have been chosen and appointed to bear fruit (John 15:16).
- I am a personal witness of Christ (Acts 1:8).
- I am God's temple (1 Corinthians 3:16).
- I am a minister of reconciliation for God (2 Corinthians 5:17-2).
- I am God's coworker (2 Corinthians 6:1, 1 Corinthians 3:9).
- I am seated with Christ in the heavenly realm (Ephesians 2:6).
- I am God's workmanship (Ephesians 2:10).
- I may approach God with freedom and confidence (Ephesians 3:12).
- I can do all things through Christ, who strengthens me (Philippians 4:13).

Taken from *Living Free in Christ* by Neil T. Anderson, published by Regal Books.

Presenting a Healthy View of Sex and Sexuality to Your Children

Paul says, "When I was a child, I talked like a child, I thought like a child, I reasoned like a child" (1 Corinthians 13:11). Children don't think like adults. They live in a convoluted world of feelings and experiences. They can misunderstand messages from authority figures and peers. It would be great if we all had perfect parents who taught us the truth about love and sex, but such is not the case. Most teenagers today have been raised in pagan and/or broken homes, and many of our Christian homes are dysfunctional. Consequently, many children are not afforded the opportunity to develop their sexuality in a God-intended way. And the effect will be felt in succeeding generations.

But however healthy or unhealthy your upbringing may have been, you have the exciting opportunity to positively impact your children and bring them up in the nurture and admonition of the Lord. This includes teaching them God's truth about sex and sexuality. Sexual development should never be seen as isolated from a child's spiritual, emotional, and mental development. We should dedicate our children to the Lord, pray for their protection, and provide the emotional support and sexual education they need to develop.

Incest is double jeopardy not only because the children are sexually violated but because their parents were the offenders. Children of incestuous parents lose their spiritual covering and protection. Nothing can be more disheartening than to be abused by the very ones who are intended by God to protect them from such abuse.

In the Scriptures, sexuality and spirituality were interrelated. The Mosaic law (Leviticus 12:2-7) required that a mother present a burnt offering and a sin offering for her cleansing after the birth of her first male child. The boy was to be circumcised on the eighth day, but the mother remained unclean for 33 more days. After Joseph and Mary had completed the days for their purification, they brought Jesus to Jerusalem to present Him to the Lord (Luke 2:22). God desires to be involved in all phases of life, including sex, pregnancy, birth, and development.

Healthy Sexual Development

Not all children develop exactly the same way, but there are several factors which should be considered essential for a child's healthy sexual development. A sense of trust should be encouraged beginning with infancy. In healthy, stable homes, emotional bonding takes place within the first nine months. Breast-feeding epitomizes the closeness of mother and child and fulfills the dependency needs every baby has. The belief that an infant boy may develop into a homosexual from over-exposure to his mother's breasts is a myth. Affectionate touch is a primary means by which a child develops emotionally. Hugs, kisses, and the genuine loving touch of parents should always be perceived by the child as an affirmation of his worth. That is why it is such an incredible violation when a parent touches a child for his or her own sexual pleasure. The child may grow up feeling dirty, and some violated children can't stand to be touched even in an affirming way.

Spanking may be used as a means to shape behavior. The intention is to shape the will by reinforcing good behavior and discouraging wrong or willfully defiant behavior by spanking. Spanking should not be viewed as punishing children for doing wrong but as discipline to keep them from doing wrong again. Punishment is retroactive, but discipline is done to superintend future choices. Hebrews 12:11 reminds us, "No discipline seems pleasant at the time, but painful. Later on, however, it produces a harvest of righteousness and peace for those who have been trained by it." Proper discipline is a proof of a parent's love. Whenever possible, use an instrument other than the hand for spanking. The hand of a parent should be extended in love. Anytime we touch another person it should be for his or her benefit.

The Exploratory Stage

Children between ages two and four are in an exploratory stage. During this time they should learn to control body eliminations, with the process only understood to be dirty by the child in reference to hygiene. Fondling the genitals, like playing with their toes or curling their hair with a finger, is normal at this stage as children explore their own body parts. Conveying adult sexual taboos and stereotypes to an innocent child will prove counterproductive. It could lead a child to distorted concepts of himself in one of two ways.

First, he could develop sexual inhibitions leading to frigidity. I think we unwittingly do this when we assign silly names to body parts, like parents who say to their child, "This is your nose, and this is your arm, and this is your waa waa." Consequently, many adults are embarrassed by words like vagina and penis because they perceive these terms as vulgar or dirty. But why should legitimate names for God-created parts of our anatomy be considered dirty?

Second, being negative during the exploratory stage could prompt a child to respond rebelliously by thinking, "I want to touch myself here. What's wrong with it?" Out of willful defiance or curiosity they begin to play with themselves secretly. Parental silence or distortions may contribute to unnatural experimentation and eventually their sexual promiscuity.

If a child is sexually violated during this time, his or her development may be distorted. I have counseled adults who have confided that they have compulsively masturbated since they were three. That is not normal development. There is a good chance someone with this problem has been sexually abused as a child.

The Questioning Stage

Questions about sex begin between ages four and five. Children at this age neither want, need, nor can they understand a comprehensive sex talk. Start by reinforcing their questions and reviewing what they already know or have heard. Again, don't project adult feelings into a child who is not ready to understand or receive them. No storks! Fantasy answers for real questions are neither healthy nor honest.

The Experimental Stage

Between ages six and ten, children begin to experiment sexually. Many children during this stage will become involved in opposite-sex exploratory play or experiences. In most cases such play is normal and seldom causes any lasting problems. An overreaction or response of horror by parents to innocent experimentation may do more damage. Nudity is an important issue at this stage. Modesty should be taught and modeled in a healthy way.

Puberty

Puberty begins between ages 11 and 13 for most children. Hormone secretion begins three years before puberty. For the female, estrogen and progesterone are very irregular until a year after puberty, and then the rhythmic monthly pattern of menstruation begins. For the male, testosterone increases at puberty and reaches its maximum at 20 years of age.

Personal touching of the genitals is no longer a soothing or comforting experience, but a means of sexual arousal. A healthy parental discussion should precede this time. A boy needs to understand why he experiences erections and seminal emissions. Otherwise, guilt and shame may be associated with a natural and pleasurable experience. A girl should fully understand what her monthly period is before she experiences her first one. She may be frightened or embarrassed if it occurs before she is prepared for it.

Dating

Your adolescent children must be taught that to treat a date as anything less than a child of God is to defile and defraud him or her. A college student under my ministry years ago was dating a lovely Christian lady. He shared with me a profound thought: "I treat my girlfriend the way I think her future husband would want her to be treated." That couple is now happily married.

Years ago I spoke at an outreach meeting to a group of high schoolers about sex. A non-Christian was there with his girlfriend. He asked, "If I had sex with my girlfriend, would I later regret it?" What a mature question. But I think there is an even more mature one he could ask: "Would my girlfriend later regret it?" Questions like these need to be lovingly discussed with your teen children before they go out on their first date.

Discipline and Spiritual Training

Prior to puberty, responsible behavior is the major objective of parenting and Christian education. Wrong behavior should be disciplined and good behavior reinforced with praise. Children should be taught what is right and wrong, and swift, cheerful obedience should be presented as their only viable option to parental directives. Rules should be clearly explained, discussed to ensure understanding, and consistently enforced in love. Rules apart from a loving relationship lead to rebellion.

Along with the physical changes of puberty, other changes are occurring in the child. His ability to reason has become fully developed. Numerous studies by Jean Piaget and other child development specialists have clearly established that the mind of an average 12-year-old is able to understand symbolism and abstract thoughts. It is interesting that the only appearance of Christ other than being an infant or an adult was when He was 12. Historically, Jewish families conduct bar mitzvahs (for boys) and bat mitzvahs (for girls) at the completion of a child's twelfth year, believing that he or she is now religiously responsible. Many liturgical churches conduct confirmation classes and ceremonies between the ages of 12 and 14. This is also understood by many to be the age of identity.

Dedication to the Lord

It is my firm belief that we should dedicate ourselves as parents and our children to the Lord soon after their birth. Then at the earliest opportunity we should lead our kids to a saving knowledge of the Lord Jesus Christ. As they approach their twelfth birthday, they need to know who they are as children of God. As parents we can't go everywhere they go, nor can we totally protect them from the harsh realities of this world. But God can and does go with them wherever they go, and He can and will protect them. This concept is discussed in greater detail in a book I wrote with Steve Russo, *The Seduction of Our Children*. The point I want to make here is that our instruction to our children during this age concerning sex needs to go far beyond behavioral objectives such as "Don't touch that," "Don't show this," and "Don't do that." Simply laying down the law won't do it. Telling them what is wrong does not give them the power to stop doing it. The law is powerless to give life: "For if a law had been given that could impart life, then righteousness would certainly have come by the law" (Galatians 3:21). Our children need to understand their feelings, the nature of their thought life, and the nature of temptation. They must have a biblical understanding of who they are, who God is, and how to relate to the opposite sex.

If our children are going to walk as children of light (Ephesians 5:8), they must first understand who they are as children of light. Right belief determines right behavior. If your child knew who he was as a child of God, would it affect the way he lives? The apostle John sure thought so. "How great is the love the Father has lavished on us, that we should be called children of God! Dear friends, now we are children of God. . . . Everyone who has this hope in him purifies himself, just as he is pure" (1 John 3:1-3). It isn't what your child does that determines who he is; who he is determines what he does. Not only will a true perspective of himself affect our child's behavior, but how he perceive others greatly determines how he treats them.

Notes

CHAPTER 1—There Is a Way Out
1. Patrick Carnes, Ph.D., *Contrary to Love* (Minneapolis: CompCare Publishers, 1989), adapted from pp. 79-85.

CHAPTER 2—The Lure of a Sex-Crazed World
1. Reported by Marilyn Elias in *USA Today* (November 8, 1993).
2. "Christian Society Today," a publication of the American Family Association, Tupelo, MS (January 1994), p. 3.

CHAPTER 3—Pathways to Sexual Bondage
1. Maxine Hancock and Karen Burton-Mains, *Child Sexual Abuse: A Hope for Healing* (Wheaton, IL: Harold Shaw Publishers, 1987), p. 12.
2. Herant A. Katchadourian, M.D. and Donald T. Lunde, M.D., *Fundamentals of Human Sexuality*, 3rd ed. (New York: Holt, Rinehart, and Winston Publishers, 1980), p. 379.
3. Barbara Chester, *Sexual Assault and Abuse* (San Francisco: Harper and Row Publishers, 1987), pp. 23-24.

CHAPTER 6—The Harvest of Sinful Deeds
1. Joe McIlhaney, *Sexuality and Sexually Transmitted Diseases* (Grand Rapids, MI: Baker Book House, 1990), p. 14.

CHAPTER 9—Behaving Must Follow Believing
1. Neil T. Anderson, *The Bondage Breaker* (Eugene, OR: Harvest House Publishers, 1990), adapted from pages 48-52.